ZELL AM

Travel Guide 2025

Discover Austria's Alpine Paradise with Breathtaking Scenery & Year-Round Adventures"

James J. Lambert

Copyright Page

© 2025

All rights reserved.

This book, including all its contents, is protected by copyright law and may not be reproduced, distributed, or transmitted in any form or by any means whether electronic, mechanical, photocopying, recording, or otherwise without the prior written permission of the copyright holder, except as permitted by applicable copyright law. Unauthorized use or reproduction of this work is strictly prohibited and may result in legal action. For permissions or inquiries, please contact the author or their representative. All rights, including those not expressly granted, are reserved.

Disclaimer

The information in this book is for general informational and entertainment purposes only. While every effort has been made to ensure accuracy, the author and publisher make no warranties, express or implied, regarding the completeness, reliability, or suitability of the content. Readers are encouraged to verify details independently before making travel plans or decisions.

The author and publisher are not responsible for any loss, injury, or inconvenience resulting from the use of this book. Any reliance on the information provided is strictly at the reader's own risk. Views expressed are those of the author and do not constitute professional advice.

TABLE OF CONTENTS

CHAPTER 1: INTRODUCTION -------- 9

    1.1 Overview of Zell am See -------- 9

    1.2 Why Visit? (Unique Attractions & Highlights) -------- 10

    1.3 Best Time to Visit (Seasonal Insights) -------- 12

    1.4 Who is This Guide For? (Families, Couples, Solo Travelers, Budget & Luxury Tourists) -------- 13

CHAPTER 2: PLANNING YOUR TRIP -------- 16

    2.1 Entry Requirements (Visa, Passport, Vaccinations) -------- 16

    2.2 Best Travel Seasons & Climate Guide -------- 18

    2.3 Recommended Duration of Stay -------- 20

    2.4 Packing List & Essentials for All Seasons -------- 21

CHAPTER 3: GETTING THERE AND AROUND -------- 24

    3.1 Best Ways to Reach the Destination (Flights, Trains, Ferries, Buses) -------- 24

    3.2 Local Transportation Guide (Taxis, Metro, Buses, Bike Rentals) -------- 28

    3.3 Navigating the City (Maps, Apps, Local Tips) -------- 30

CHAPTER 4: WHERE TO STAY -------- 32

    4.1 Best Neighborhoods for Tourists -------- 32

    4.2 Budget Accommodations (Hostels, Guesthouses, Affordable Hotels) -------- 34

    4.3 Mid-Range & Boutique Hotels -------- 36

    4.4 Luxury Hotels & Resorts -------- 37

    4.5 Unique Stays (Eco-Lodges, Airbnb, Historical Properties) -------- 38

CHAPTER 5: TOP ATTRACTIONS & MUST-SEE LANDMARKS -------- 41

    5.1 Iconic Landmarks & Historical Sites -------- 41

    5.2 Museums & Cultural Centers -------- 43

    5.3 Natural Wonders (Beaches, Mountains, Lakes, National Parks) -------- 44

    5.4 Best Viewpoints & Photography Spots -------- 46

CHAPTER 6: HIDDEN GEMS & OFF-THE-BEATEN-PATH EXPERIENCES -------- 49

    6.1 Lesser-Known Attractions & Local Secrets -------- 49

    6.2 Underrated Neighborhoods & Villages -------- 51

6.3 Unique Experiences Not Found in Typical Guides --- 53

CHAPTER 7: FOOD & DRINKS: A CULINARY JOURNEY --- 56

7.1 Traditional Dishes to Try --- 56

7.2 Best Restaurants & Street Food Vendors --- 58

7.3 Cafés, Bars & Local Nightlife --- 60

7.4 Food Markets & Culinary Tours --- 62

CHAPTER 8: SHOPPING & SOUVENIRS --- 64

8.1 Best Shopping Districts & Malls --- 64

8.2 Local Handicrafts, Art & Artisanal Goods --- 66

8.3 Budget-Friendly Shopping vs. Luxury Boutiques --- 68

CHAPTER 9: OUTDOOR ADVENTURES & ACTIVITIES --- 72

9.1 Hiking, Biking, and Walking Tours --- 72

9.2 Water Activities (Snorkeling, Diving, Boat Cruises) --- 74

9.3 Wildlife Experiences & Eco-Tourism --- 76

9.4 Extreme Sports & Adventure Activities --- 78

CHAPTER 10: CULTURAL EXPERIENCES & LOCAL TRADITIONS --- 80

10.1 Understanding Local Customs & Etiquette --- 80

10.2 Festivals & Traditional Celebrations --- 82

10.3 Music, Dance, and Art Scene --- 84

10.4 Historical Influences on the Culture --- 85

CHAPTER 11: SEASONAL TRAVEL GUIDE --- 88

11.1 Visiting in Spring (March – May) --- 88

11.2 Summer Adventures (June – August) --- 90

11.3 Autumn Charm (September – November) --- 92

11.4 Winter Wonderland (December – February) --- 93

CHAPTER 12: ITINERARIES FOR EVERY TYPE OF TRAVELER --- 96

12.1 24-Hour Express Itinerary --- 96

12.2 3-Day Classic Itinerary --- 97

12.3 7-Day In-Depth Itinerary --- 100

12.4 Family-Friendly Itinerary ---------- 101
12.5 Romantic Getaway for Couples ---------- 102
12.6 Budget Traveler's Itinerary ---------- 103
12.7 Luxury & VIP Experience Itinerary ---------- 104

CHAPTER 13: DAY TRIPS & NEARBY EXCURSIONS ---------- 106

13.1 Best Nearby Towns & Cities to Visit ---------- 106
13.2 Scenic Road Trips & Train Journeys ---------- 108
13.3 Island Hopping & Coastal Escapes ---------- 111

CHAPTER 14: NIGHTLIFE & ENTERTAINMENT ---------- 113

14.1 Best Bars, Clubs, and Lounges ---------- 113
14.2 Live Music & Theaters ---------- 115
14.3 Unique Nighttime Experiences ---------- 117

CHAPTER 15: TRAVEL TIPS & SAFETY GUIDE ---------- 121

15.1 Local Laws & Travel Regulations ---------- 121
15.2 Common Scams & Tourist Traps to Avoid ---------- 123
15.3 Emergency Contacts & Medical Facilities ---------- 125
15.4 Must-Have Apps & Local Services ---------- 127

CHAPTER 16: BUDGETING & MONEY MATTERS ---------- 130

16.1 Currency Exchange & Payment Options ---------- 130
16.2 Cost of Living & Budget Breakdown ---------- 132
16.3 Saving Money & Travel Hacks ---------- 136

CHAPTER 17: LUXURY TRAVEL & EXCLUSIVE EXPERIENCES ---------- 139

17.1 High-End Hotels & Resorts ---------- 139
17.2 Private Tours & VIP Access ---------- 141
17.3 Michelin-Star Restaurants & Fine Dining ---------- 143

CHAPTER 18: SOLO TRAVELER'S GUIDE ---------- 147

18.1 Safety Tips & Precautions ---------- 147
18.2 Best Places for Solo Travelers ---------- 149
18.3 How to Meet Fellow Travelers & Locals ---------- 152

CHAPTER 19: FAMILY & KID-FRIENDLY TRAVEL — 155

- 19.1 Best Attractions for Kids — 155
- 19.2 Family-Friendly Accommodations & Restaurants — 158
- 19.3 Tips for Traveling with Children — 160

CHAPTER 20: SUSTAINABLE & RESPONSIBLE TOURISM — 163

- 20.1 Eco-Friendly Accommodations & Tours — 163
- 20.2 Supporting Local Communities & Ethical Tourism — 166
- 20.3 Reducing Your Environmental Impact — 168

CHAPTER 21: PHOTOGRAPHY & SOCIAL MEDIA HOTSPOTS — 171

- 21.1 Most Instagrammable Locations — 171
- 21.2 Best Times & Angles for Capturing Stunning Photos — 174
- 21.3 Photography Tours & Workshops — 176

CHAPTER 22: WHAT TO AVOID & COMMON TRAVEL MISTAKES — 179

- 22.1 Overpriced Attractions & Tourist Traps — 179
- 22.2 Cultural Taboos & Mistakes to Avoid — 181
- 22.3 Travel Mishaps & How to Prevent Them — 183

CHAPTER 23: DEPARTURE & FINAL TRAVEL TIPS — 187

- 23.1 Last-Minute Shopping & Packing Checklist — 187
- 23.2 Getting to the Airport or Train Station — 190
- 23.3 Making the Most of Your Final Day — 191

CHAPTER 24: APPENDIX & ADDITIONAL RESOURCES — 194

- 24.1 Recommended Books, Websites & Travel Blogs — 194
- 24.2 Essential Phrases in the Local Language — 196
- 24.3 Emergency Contacts & Local Helplines — 197
- 24.4 Addresses of Major Landmarks, Attractions, and Important Locations — 198
- 24.5 Local Holidays & Festivals Calendar — 200
- 24.6 Helpful Travel Apps and Websites — 201

General Map Of Zell am See

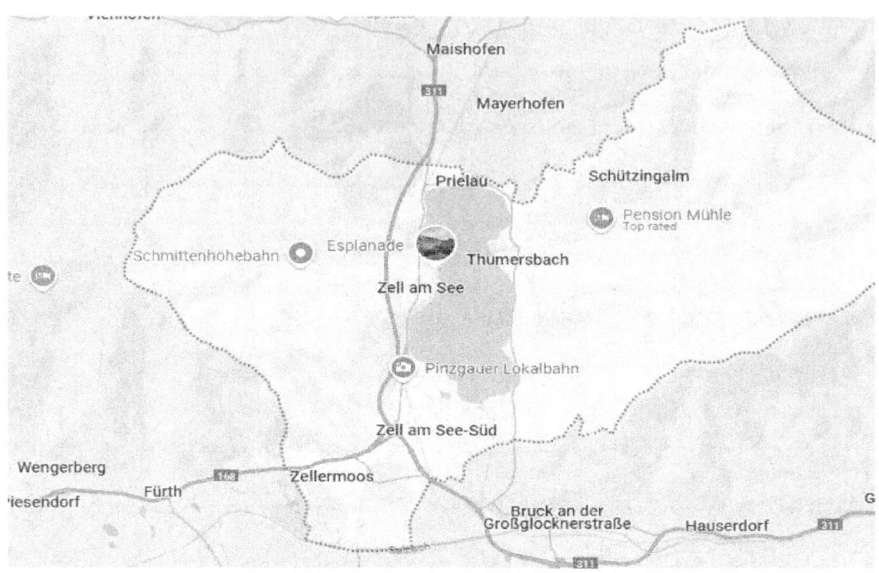

https://maps.app.goo.gl/tpPuxk5ESLmk2Lkk7

Scan the QR-Code to see the real time location

Chapter 1: Introduction

Zell am See is one of Austria's hidden gems, a place where the natural world and small-town charm converge in the most spectacular of ways. Nestled in the heart of the Austrian Alps, this idyllic lakeside town offers visitors an unparalleled escape whether you're seeking adventure, relaxation, or a little bit of both. Here, snow-capped peaks meet crystal-clear waters, and history lingers in every cobbled street. With its diverse appeal, Zell am See invites travelers from all walks of life to experience the essence of Austrian beauty.

1.1 Overview of Zell am See

Zell am See, located in the state of Salzburg, is a postcard-perfect town sitting beside the shimmering waters of Lake Zell. Surrounded by majestic alpine peaks, the town offers both tranquility and adventure, blending outdoor experiences with cultural richness. From winter sports on the Kitzsteinhorn glacier to serene summer days spent hiking, cycling, or simply strolling along the lake, Zell am See caters to all kinds of travelers.

The town's medieval center, with its charming streets, cozy cafes, and vibrant market squares, provides a glimpse into its storied past.

Zell am See has a long history that dates back to Roman times, but it's best known for its strategic location between the towering peaks and the lake, making it a prime destination for both adventure-seekers and those wanting a quiet retreat in nature.

A place of contrasts, Zell am See effortlessly balances modern luxury with traditional charm. Whether you're sipping coffee at a lakeside café or hiking to the summit of the nearby mountains, the town radiates a warm, inviting energy that makes every traveler feel at home.

1.2 Why Visit? (Unique Attractions & Highlights)

If you're wondering what sets Zell am See apart from other alpine destinations, the answer lies in the stunning combination of natural beauty and outdoor adventure. From skiing in winter to hiking, cycling, and boat trips in the warmer months, Zell am See offers endless opportunities for exploration.

- **Lake Zell**: A tranquil, crystal-clear lake with views so striking you'll want to pinch yourself. Whether you're taking a boat tour, enjoying the shores, or just gazing out at the landscape, the lake's charm is undeniable. During the summer, it's a haven for swimmers, paddleboarders, and those who enjoy the refreshing mountain air.

- **Kitzsteinhorn Glacier**: Year-round skiing and snowboarding await at this iconic glacier. The glacier is accessible even in the warmer months, offering spectacular views of the surrounding mountains and a taste of Austria's premier winter sports culture.

- **Schmittenhöhe**: For hiking enthusiasts, Schmittenhöhe is the place to be. The panoramic views from the summit are nothing short of breathtaking. Whether you're hiking or riding the cable car, you'll find yourself surrounded by alpine scenery that seems almost too perfect to be real.

- **Zell am See Old Town**: A charming walk through the town center is an experience in itself. Narrow lanes, old-town charm, quaint shops, and traditional cafés await you, along with local markets selling handmade goods and regional delicacies.

- **The Tauern Spa**: A luxurious escape, especially after a day of skiing or hiking. This wellness center is perfect for those looking to unwind with stunning alpine views and a range of spa treatments that will melt away any stress.

These are just a few of the highlights that make Zell am See an unmissable destination, but the town has much more to offer, whether it's your first visit or your tenth.

1.3 Best Time to Visit (Seasonal Insights)

Zell am See is a year-round destination, and the best time to visit depends largely on the type of experience you're looking for. Every season in Zell am See brings a new layer of beauty and adventure.

- **Winter (December to February)**: If you're a fan of winter sports, this is undoubtedly the best time to visit. Zell am See turns into a winter wonderland, with snow-capped mountains perfect for skiing and snowboarding. The festive Christmas markets are a highlight during this time, offering a magical atmosphere with twinkling lights, mulled wine, and local handicrafts. The Kitzsteinhorn glacier ensures that snow is almost guaranteed for the entire season.

- **Spring (March to May)**: Spring is a beautiful time to visit, especially if you love seeing nature come alive. The weather starts to warm up, and the snow on the lower slopes melts, leaving behind lush green meadows. It's a quieter time to explore, and the trails around the lake are perfect for scenic walks. This is also the perfect time for a slower pace and an opportunity to experience Zell am See without the hustle and bustle of peak tourist season.

- **Summer (June to August)**: Summer in Zell am See is the most active season, with the lake coming alive for swimming, boating, and water sports. Temperatures are ideal for hiking and biking in the surrounding mountains. It's the perfect time to enjoy outdoor dining, with many restaurants offering terrace seating to take in the spectacular views. Summer also brings various festivals, such as the Zell am See Music Festival, which is a treat for music lovers.

- **Autumn (September to November)**: Fall is when Zell am See truly shows its colors. The surrounding forests turn into a riot of reds, oranges, and golds, making hiking and biking a magical experience. The crowds thin out, and the weather remains mild, so it's an excellent time for those who want to experience Zell am See in a more tranquil, reflective atmosphere.

1.4 Who is This Guide For? (Families, Couples, Solo Travelers, Budget & Luxury Tourists)

This guide is designed for anyone eager to experience the stunning beauty and adventure of Zell am See, no matter your travel style or budget.

- **Families**: With its peaceful lakeside setting and family-friendly activities like boat rides, easy hikes, and visits to local parks, Zell am See is a wonderful destination for families. Kids will love swimming in the lake during summer and building snowmen in winter, while parents can enjoy the slower pace and the many local attractions.

- **Couples**: For couples looking for romance, Zell am See is ideal. Whether you're enjoying a lakeside sunset, indulging in a couples' spa experience, or sharing a romantic meal in one of the town's cozy restaurants, Zell am See offers the perfect blend of tranquility and adventure.

- **Solo Travelers**: If you're traveling alone, Zell am See's laid-back atmosphere and its wealth of outdoor activities make it a perfect choice. You'll meet fellow travelers on the trails, at local events, or in the charming town square. The town's peaceful setting also provides ample opportunities for solo reflection by the lake or in the surrounding mountains.

- **Budget Travelers**: Zell am See is more affordable than many think. There are a range of budget-friendly accommodations, from hostels and guesthouses to local inns. Public transport and bike rentals are reasonably priced, and you can experience much of the natural beauty of the area without breaking the bank.

- **Luxury Seekers**: For those who want a more opulent experience, Zell am See doesn't disappoint. From luxury hotels with alpine views to private skiing experiences on the Kitzsteinhorn glacier, there's plenty to indulge in. Fine dining, exclusive spa treatments, and tailor-made experiences await the discerning traveler.

No matter what type of traveler you are, Zell am See has something special to offer, and this guide will help you navigate it all whether you're seeking a peaceful retreat, an adventurous getaway, or a luxurious escape.

This is just the beginning of your journey into the heart of Zell am See. Let's dive deeper into the treasures of this remarkable destination!

Chapter 2: Planning Your Trip

Before you pack your bags and head to the breathtaking town of Zell am See, there are a few things you'll want to know to ensure a smooth and seamless journey. Whether it's navigating the entry requirements or figuring out what to bring, proper planning can make all the difference. In this chapter, I'll guide you through the essentials of planning your trip to Zell am See from entry requirements to the best time to visit and everything you'll need for an unforgettable stay.

2.1 Entry Requirements (Visa, Passport, Vaccinations)

For most international travelers, Zell am See is easy to reach, but it's essential to check a few key details before you embark. Austria is part of the Schengen Area, meaning that if you're traveling from another Schengen country, you won't need to go through border controls. However, if you're arriving from outside the area, there are a few things to keep in mind:

- **Visa Requirements**: Depending on your nationality, you may need a visa to enter Austria. Citizens of the European Union (EU) and European Economic Area (EEA) countries can travel freely within Austria.

For citizens of other countries, a short-stay Schengen visa is typically required for visits up to 90 days. It's a good idea to check the Austrian embassy or consulate in your home country for specific visa requirements before you travel.

- **Passport**: Ensure that your passport is valid for at least three months beyond your planned date of departure from Austria. If your passport is close to expiring, you may not be allowed to enter the country.

- **Vaccinations**: While Austria does not have specific vaccination requirements for most visitors, it's always best to check the latest health advisories before traveling. For those arriving from areas where diseases such as yellow fever are present, a vaccination certificate may be required. It's a good idea to check with your healthcare provider or local travel clinic to ensure you are up to date on general vaccinations (such as tetanus, hepatitis, etc.).

Travel Tip: Always carry a copy of your important documents, including your passport, travel insurance, and any medical prescriptions you may need while abroad. This can help you avoid unnecessary stress in case of an emergency.

2.2 Best Travel Seasons & Climate Guide

The beauty of Zell am See is that it offers something for every traveler, no matter when you visit. The climate is typical of an alpine town, with distinct seasons that bring out the charm of the region in different ways. Here's a guide to help you decide the best time to visit, depending on your preferences and travel style.

- **Winter (December to February)**: If you're drawn to snowy landscapes and winter sports, then Zell am See in winter is nothing short of magical. Temperatures can dip below freezing, especially in the higher elevations, but the town becomes a winter wonderland. Skiers and snowboarders flock to the Kitzsteinhorn glacier for snow year-round, while cozy chalets, hot chocolate by the fire, and festive Christmas markets make Zell am See a dreamy winter retreat.

- **Spring (March to May)**: Spring in Zell am See brings a lovely freshness to the region, with snow beginning to melt and flowers starting to bloom. Temperatures range from cool to mild, so it's a good time for hiking and exploring the natural beauty of the area without the summer crowds. Spring is a fantastic time to visit if you want to see the town come alive as the warmer weather begins to settle in.

- **Summer (June to August)**: This is the high season for Zell am See, and for good reason. Summer brings warmth and an abundance of outdoor activities, from boating and swimming on Lake Zell to hiking and cycling in the surrounding mountains. The weather is typically mild and sunny, with temperatures reaching into the 70s (Fahrenheit), making it ideal for enjoying all that Zell am See has to offer. Summer also means festivals, outdoor concerts, and a vibrant town atmosphere.

- **Autumn (September to November)**: Autumn is arguably one of the best-kept secrets in Zell am See. The crowds thin out, the air is crisp, and the autumn colors transform the landscape into a stunning canvas of reds, yellows, and oranges. It's a quieter time to visit, perfect for those seeking a more peaceful and introspective experience. If you're a fan of hiking, this is a wonderful time to explore the many trails while enjoying the fall foliage.

Travel Tip: Regardless of when you visit, the weather can change quickly in the mountains. Be sure to pack layers and always be prepared for sudden shifts in temperature.

2.3 Recommended Duration of Stay

Zell am See is small enough that you can explore much of it in a few days, but there's also enough to do to keep you entertained for a longer stay. Depending on your travel style and interests, here's a breakdown of how long you might want to stay:

- **Short Stay (2-3 Days)**: If you're limited on time, Zell am See can be easily explored in a short stay. You'll have time to visit the main attractions, take a boat ride on the lake, and enjoy a couple of hikes. A weekend stay is perfect for those who want to get a taste of Zell am See's alpine charm without a long commitment.

- **Mid-Length Stay (4-5 Days)**: A longer stay allows you to dive deeper into Zell am See's offerings. You'll have time for multiple outdoor activities, perhaps even a day on the slopes or a longer hiking excursion. You can also explore nearby attractions like the Kitzsteinhorn glacier or the Tauern Spa, and still have time to relax and enjoy the town's laid-back atmosphere.

- **Extended Stay (1 Week or More)**: If you're an outdoor enthusiast, you'll find plenty to keep you occupied for a full week or longer.

From skiing and snowboarding in winter to hiking, biking, and water activities in summer, a longer stay allows you to experience Zell am See in a more leisurely way. It's also a great opportunity to take day trips to nearby towns and cities, such as Salzburg or the Grossglockner High Alpine Road.

Travel Tip: If you're planning to visit during peak seasons like summer or winter, consider booking your accommodations in advance, as Zell am See can get quite busy. For a more relaxed visit, spring or autumn is ideal.

2.4 Packing List & Essentials for All Seasons

Packing for Zell am See largely depends on the time of year you're visiting, but there are some essentials you'll want to bring no matter when you arrive. The weather can be unpredictable, so it's always wise to be prepared for all conditions.

- **Winter (December to February)**:
    - Warm layers (thermal tops, fleece, down jacket)
    - Waterproof and insulated boots for snow
    - Ski gear (if you're planning to hit the slopes)
    - Gloves, scarves, and hats to protect against the cold
    - Sunglasses or goggles (snow glare can be intense)

- Sunscreen (yes, even in winter the sun can be strong in the mountains)

- **Spring & Autumn (March to May, September to November)**:
    - Layered clothing for variable temperatures
    - Waterproof jacket or windbreaker (it can rain unexpectedly)
    - Comfortable shoes for hiking and walking
    - Light sweaters or long-sleeve shirts
    - A good pair of sunglasses
    - A small backpack for daily excursions

- **Summer (June to August)**:
    - Lightweight and breathable clothing for warmth
    - Hiking boots or comfortable walking shoes
    - Swimwear for lake activities
    - A hat and sunscreen for protection against the sun
    - A light jacket for cooler evenings

Travel Tip: If you plan on hiking or skiing, don't forget to bring specialized gear like walking poles, ski goggles, or a daypack. Renting equipment is an option, but if you're going for multiple activities, it can be more economical to bring your own.

Now that you're fully prepared for your adventure to Zell am See, it's time to immerse yourself in the stunning beauty of this alpine paradise. Whether you're here for the adventure, the culture, or the peace of nature, Zell am See is sure to provide an unforgettable experience. With this practical guide in hand, you'll navigate the essentials with ease, leaving you free to enjoy all that this magnificent destination has to offer.

Chapter 3: Getting There and Around

One of the greatest joys of traveling to Zell am See is its accessibility whether you prefer the ease of a flight, the scenic charm of a train journey, or the adventure of a road trip, Zell am See is welcoming, no matter how you arrive. In this chapter, I'll guide you through the best ways to reach Zell am See, how to get around once you're there, and the little local tips that will make your travel experience even more enjoyable. By the time you finish this chapter, you'll be ready to start your adventure smoothly and with confidence.

3.1 Best Ways to Reach the Destination (Flights, Trains, Ferries, Buses)

Zell am See may feel like a tucked-away gem in the heart of Austria's Alps, but it's surprisingly easy to get to from several major cities in Europe. Whether you're coming from a nearby country or arriving from farther afield, here are the most convenient options to consider.

- **By Air**: Zell am See doesn't have its own airport, but don't worry there are several major airports within a short distance, making the town easy to reach by plane.

- **Salzburg Airport (SZG)**: Located about 80 kilometers (50 miles) away from Zell am See, Salzburg is the closest international airport. From here, you can catch a train or a bus to Zell am See in about 1.5 hours. The airport serves flights from major European cities, making it an ideal choice for visitors from across the continent.

- **Munich Airport (MUC)**: For international travelers, Munich's airport is a major hub, located approximately 200 kilometers (124 miles) from Zell am See. The drive from Munich to Zell am See takes around 2.5 to 3 hours. Alternatively, you can take a train directly from Munich to Zell am See in about 2.5 hours, which offers a scenic and comfortable journey.

- **Innsbruck Airport (INN)**: Situated around 150 kilometers (93 miles) away, Innsbruck offers another option for those flying into Austria. Though a bit farther than Salzburg, it's an excellent choice for travelers already in western Austria or southern Germany.

Travel Tip: For flights, try to book in advance to snag the best deals, especially if you're visiting during the peak summer or winter months.

- **By Train**: The train system in Austria is one of the most efficient and scenic ways to travel, and Zell am See is well-connected to several cities across the country. The main train station in Zell am See is just a short walk from the town center and offers direct routes from places like Salzburg, Vienna, and Munich.

  - **From Salzburg**: If you're flying into Salzburg, the train journey to Zell am See is a picturesque one, winding through the alpine landscapes. The journey takes just under two hours, and trains depart regularly throughout the day.

  - **From Vienna**: If you're coming from Austria's capital, you'll catch a direct train from Vienna Hauptbahnhof (Main Station) to Zell am See. The trip takes about 4.5 hours, but it's a comfortable and scenic ride through the Austrian countryside.

Travel Tip: Trains are known for being punctual, but always check the schedules ahead of time, especially if you're traveling in the off-season when schedules can change.

- **By Bus**: If you're looking for an affordable and convenient option, buses to Zell am See are readily available. Several bus companies, including FlixBus, offer long-distance routes connecting major cities to Zell am See. Though the journey may take longer than the train, buses are a great budget-friendly option for those traveling on a tight budget.

Travel Tip: Booking bus tickets in advance online can save you money and guarantee a seat.

- **By Car**: Renting a car gives you the flexibility to explore not only Zell am See but also the stunning surrounding areas at your own pace. The town is located near major highways, and the drive from Salzburg or Munich is both scenic and easy. If you're coming from nearby destinations like the Grossglockner High Alpine Road or Salzburg, renting a car will allow you to take your time and enjoy the journey.

Travel Tip: Parking in Zell am See can be limited in peak seasons, so check with your accommodation ahead of time to ensure they offer parking or look for nearby parking lots.

3.2 Local Transportation Guide (Taxis, Metro, Buses, Bike Rentals)

Once you've arrived in Zell am See, getting around the town and the surrounding area is easy. Though Zell am See is small, there are still a variety of transportation options available, each suited to different needs.

- **Taxis**: Taxis are readily available in Zell am See and can be a convenient option for getting from the train station to your hotel or if you're heading out for a special activity. Though taxis are relatively affordable within the town, they can be more expensive if you're traveling to nearby areas or attractions. It's always a good idea to ask for an estimated fare before you get in.

Travel Tip: Use local taxi apps to call a cab if you're in a pinch, as they tend to be reliable and available for quick trips.

- **Public Buses**: Zell am See has an excellent bus system that connects the town with nearby attractions and villages. Buses are an affordable and practical option for getting to areas that are further away, like the Kitzsteinhorn glacier or the nearby town of Kaprun. Schedules are available at the bus station, and tickets can be purchased on board or from local kiosks.

Travel Tip: If you're planning to take several buses during your stay, inquire about multi-day passes or discount cards that offer unlimited travel within the area.

- **Bike Rentals**: Zell am See is an outdoor lover's dream, and one of the best ways to explore the town and its surroundings is by bike. There are plenty of bike rental shops throughout the town, offering everything from standard bikes to e-bikes for those who want a little extra assistance on the hills. The town is bike-friendly, with scenic paths along the lake and through the mountains.

Travel Tip: If you're planning to rent a bike, check out the surrounding bike routes. One of my favorites is the route around Lake Zell, which offers stunning views and an easy ride.

- **Car Rentals**: If you're planning to venture outside of Zell am See, renting a car is the most convenient option. While the town itself is walkable, having a car gives you access to nearby attractions such as the nearby Grossglockner High Alpine Road, Salzburg, or the charming towns in the nearby Pinzgau Valley.

Travel Tip: Be sure to familiarize yourself with local road rules before renting a car. While driving in Austria is relatively straightforward, mountain roads can be tricky, especially in winter.

3.3 Navigating the City (Maps, Apps, Local Tips)

Navigating Zell am See is straightforward, and there are a few key tools and tips that will make your trip even more enjoyable.

- **Maps & Guides**: Zell am See is small, and its layout is easy to navigate on foot. However, it's still helpful to have a map or guide to help you locate specific spots. The town's tourist information center offers free maps of the area, which you can pick up upon arrival.

Travel Tip: Download a map of Zell am See to your phone in case you find yourself without Wi-Fi. There are also several local hiking maps available for purchase if you plan on exploring the surrounding mountains.

- **Mobile Apps**: There are several apps that can make your trip easier. For transportation, the ÖBB (Austrian Federal Railways) app provides up-to-date information on trains, buses, and schedules. For a more in-depth guide to the town, try apps like Google Maps, which will give you walking and driving directions, and Komoot, which specializes in outdoor activities and hiking routes.

Travel Tip: Many places in Zell am See offer free Wi-Fi, but it's always good to have a local SIM card or a portable hotspot for internet access when you're outside of town.

- **Local Tips**:
    - Zell am See is incredibly walkable, and many of the attractions are within walking distance of each other.
    - Locals are friendly and always happy to help with directions if you get lost, so don't hesitate to ask.
    - If you're heading into the mountains or hiking, be sure to pack sturdy footwear and always check the weather forecast. Alpine conditions can change quickly, especially in the higher elevations.

Getting to Zell am See and navigating your way around is simpler than you might think. Whether you're traveling by plane, train, or car, the journey is part of the adventure. Once you arrive, you'll find that Zell am See is an easy town to explore on foot, by bike, or with the help of the local bus system. And with a little local knowledge and a few helpful apps, you'll be navigating the area like a pro in no time.

Chapter 4: Where to Stay

Zell am See, nestled in the heart of Austria's breathtaking Alps, offers a variety of accommodation options, from cozy guesthouses to luxurious lakeside resorts. Whether you're a budget-conscious traveler or seeking a lavish escape, the town's diverse range of places to stay caters to every need. In this chapter, I'll walk you through the best neighborhoods, suggest the most affordable spots for budget travelers, offer recommendations for those looking for boutique-style charm, and reveal some luxurious gems for those with a taste for elegance. I'll also introduce you to unique stays that will give you a memorable and personalized experience. Get ready to find the perfect place to call home during your Zell am See adventure.

4.1 Best Neighborhoods for Tourists

Zell am See is a compact and walkable town, but its distinct neighborhoods offer different vibes and experiences. Whether you prefer being in the heart of the action or closer to nature, there's a neighborhood for everyone.

- **Zell am See Town Center**: If you want to be at the center of it all, staying in the town center is the perfect choice.

Here, you're close to the train station, restaurants, shops, and the beautiful shores of Lake Zell. It's the ideal base for those who want to explore the town's historic landmarks, enjoy lakeside walks, and have easy access to public transportation. The pedestrian-friendly streets are lined with charming cafés and boutiques, and the town's historical flair is apparent in the architecture.

- **Schüttdorf**: Just south of the town center, Schüttdorf offers a quieter, more relaxed atmosphere, with easy access to the lake and the nearby mountains. It's a great option for families or those who want a peaceful retreat but still want to be close to the town's main attractions. In winter, Schüttdorf is an excellent base for skiing enthusiasts, as it's located near the base of the Schmittenhöhe ski area.

- **Kaprun**: While technically a neighboring village, Kaprun is just a short drive or bus ride from Zell am See. It's known for its proximity to the Kitzsteinhorn Glacier and is a haven for those looking for year-round outdoor activities like skiing, snowboarding, and hiking. Staying here offers a more laid-back atmosphere compared to the town center, and it's a great option for adventurers who want easy access to the mountains.

- **Lake Zell**: Staying along the shores of Lake Zell gives you the most picturesque experience. Imagine waking up to views of the snow-capped mountains reflecting off the crystal-clear water. Whether you're staying in the center or at a resort a little farther out, the serene beauty of the lake will be a constant companion. Perfect for those who appreciate tranquility, outdoor water activities, and unparalleled natural beauty.

4.2 Budget Accommodations (Hostels, Guesthouses, Affordable Hotels)

Zell am See offers an array of affordable options without sacrificing comfort or quality. For budget travelers, the following accommodations provide the best value for money:

- **Hostels**:
    - **Jugendherberge Zell am See**: This friendly and affordable hostel is perfect for backpackers or those looking to meet fellow travelers. Located near the train station and just a short walk from the lake, it offers basic yet clean rooms and a communal atmosphere that's ideal for socializing. The on-site kitchen is great for preparing your own meals, saving you money during your stay.

- **Guesthouses**:
    - **Pension Bergland**: Situated on a quiet street, this family-run guesthouse offers an authentic Austrian experience with warm hospitality. It's a great budget-friendly option that still provides personalized service and comfortable rooms with lovely views of the mountains. Breakfast is included, and the hosts can provide you with tips on local hikes and places to visit.

- **Affordable Hotels**:
    - **Hotel Tirolerhof**: This 3-star hotel offers excellent value for money, with spacious rooms, a sauna, and an included breakfast. Its central location is a bonus, making it easy to explore Zell am See's historic center and the nearby lake. While it's not the cheapest option, its amenities and proximity to key attractions make it a great choice for those who want a little extra comfort without breaking the bank.

Travel Tip: Book early during peak seasons (summer and winter) to ensure availability at affordable prices.

4.3 Mid-Range & Boutique Hotels

If you're looking for something a bit more stylish without going overboard, Zell am See offers several mid-range and boutique hotels that strike a perfect balance between comfort and luxury.

- **Hotel Salzburgerhof**: A charming boutique hotel that combines traditional Austrian hospitality with modern comfort. Located near the lake, Hotel Salzburgerhof boasts stunning mountain views, a wellness area with a sauna and spa, and a gourmet restaurant serving regional delicacies. It's the perfect choice for those who want a bit of luxury without the price tag of a five-star hotel.

- **Grand Hotel Zell am See**: This iconic hotel is an elegant and historic property with a prime location right on the shores of Lake Zell. It has been welcoming guests for over a century and offers sophisticated rooms, an indoor pool, and an exceptional restaurant with panoramic lake views. Whether you're traveling for romance or relaxation, this grand hotel is sure to impress.

- **Seehotel Bellevue**: Offering spectacular views over Lake Zell, Seehotel Bellevue is a perfect blend of comfort and style.

With rooms that have balconies overlooking the lake and the mountains, it's ideal for couples or those looking for a romantic getaway. The hotel also has a beautiful wellness area, perfect for unwinding after a day of exploration.

Travel Tip: Look out for packages that include spa access, meals, or even ski passes in the winter months.

4.4 Luxury Hotels & Resorts

For those who prefer to indulge in the finest accommodations, Zell am See offers some exquisite luxury hotels and resorts that will make your stay truly unforgettable.

- **Schlosshotel Fuschl**: Located just outside of Zell am See, this fairytale castle hotel offers an exclusive experience. With its stunning lakeside setting, world-class amenities, and historical charm, it's perfect for those who want a luxurious retreat in the Alps. Guests can enjoy a spa, fine dining, and a range of outdoor activities such as boating and hiking.

- **The Zell am See Hotel**: This five-star luxury hotel is a true gem, offering top-tier service, fine dining, and spa treatments to ensure that you have a perfect stay. Located in the heart of the town, the hotel boasts sophisticated rooms with modern comforts.

- The highlight is its lakeside terrace, where you can enjoy a glass of Austrian wine while watching the sunset over the mountains.

- **Kempinski Hotel Das Tirol**: Situated in nearby Jochberg, this resort is a true haven for those seeking ultimate relaxation and outdoor luxury. The hotel offers ski-in, ski-out access to the slopes in the winter and luxurious rooms with incredible views of the Alps. The extensive spa facilities and gourmet restaurants make this the perfect choice for those looking to pamper themselves.

Travel Tip: During the ski season, book your stay well in advance to secure the best rooms, as these luxury resorts fill up quickly.

4.5 Unique Stays (Eco-Lodges, Airbnb, Historical Properties)

For travelers who seek something different or more personal, Zell am See offers a few unique accommodation experiences that make your stay unforgettable.

- **Eco-Lodges & Sustainable Stays**:
  - **Zell am See Eco Lodge**: Located on the outskirts of town, this eco-friendly lodge emphasizes sustainability without compromising on comfort.

Powered by renewable energy, the lodge uses natural materials and offers an organic, nature-based experience. It's ideal for those who want to enjoy a peaceful retreat while reducing their carbon footprint.

- **Airbnb**: If you prefer a home-away-from-home experience, Zell am See has numerous charming Airbnb properties, from lakeside apartments with stunning views to cozy mountain chalets. Staying in an Airbnb offers a unique opportunity to immerse yourself in the local community and experience Zell am See from a more personal perspective.

- **Historical Properties**:
    - **Villa Seilern**: This historic villa, dating back to the early 1900s, combines old-world charm with modern amenities. It offers a variety of rooms and apartments, each one filled with character. Located a short distance from the lake, it's the perfect place for history buffs who want to stay in a property with stories to tell.

Travel Tip: If you're planning on booking an Airbnb or a unique stay, always check reviews for hidden gems, as they can provide personal insights and tips that you won't find in the guidebooks.

No matter your budget or style of travel, Zell am See offers a variety of accommodations to ensure your stay is as comfortable, enjoyable, and memorable as possible. From charming guesthouses to luxurious lakeside resorts, you'll find a place that suits your needs, allowing you to fully immerse yourself in this beautiful Alpine town. Whether you prefer to wake up to the sound of birds chirping by the lake or the hustle and bustle of the town center, Zell am See has something for everyone.

Chapter 5: Top Attractions & Must-See Landmarks

Zell am See, nestled in the heart of the Austrian Alps, is a destination that captivates the senses with its perfect blend of natural beauty, rich history, and cultural allure. Whether you're a history enthusiast, an outdoor adventurer, or simply someone looking to relax by the lake, Zell am See offers an abundance of attractions and landmarks that promise to make your visit unforgettable. In this chapter, I'll guide you through the most iconic landmarks, cultural hotspots, natural wonders, and stunning viewpoints, each one offering a unique glimpse into the soul of this charming Alpine town.

5.1 Iconic Landmarks & Historical Sites

Zell am See is steeped in history, and its landmarks tell the stories of centuries past. From the medieval to the modern, here are the must-see historical sites that provide a glimpse into the town's rich heritage.

- **Stadtplatz (Town Square)**: The heart of Zell am See is its charming Town Square, a picturesque spot surrounded by colorful buildings, cafés, and shops. Here, you'll find the beautiful St.

Hippolyte's Church, an iconic piece of Gothic architecture dating back to the 14th century. Its tall spire dominates the town's skyline, and inside, you'll discover remarkable frescoes and intricate details that tell the story of Zell am See's past. The square itself is often bustling with life, and it's the perfect place to start your exploration.

- **Zell am See Castle (Schloss Zell am See)**: This historic castle, dating back to the 12th century, stands proudly by the shores of Lake Zell. Once a noble residence, it now houses a museum and a gallery. The castle's impressive façade and its picturesque setting against the backdrop of the lake and mountains make it one of the most photogenic landmarks in the area. A walk through its halls and grounds is like stepping back in time, with the castle's rich history unfolding around you.

- **Kaprun Castle (Schloss Kaprun)**: A short drive from Zell am See, the medieval Kaprun Castle is a stunning example of an Austrian fortress. Built in the 12th century, this well-preserved castle offers panoramic views of the surrounding mountains. Inside, you can explore its exhibits on local history, including medieval armor and artifacts. The castle's location above the town offers a fascinating perspective of the Alpine landscape.

Travel Tip: Check the opening hours before visiting, as some historical sites in the region are seasonal and may close during the off-peak months.

5.2 Museums & Cultural Centers

For those looking to dive deeper into the history and culture of Zell am See and the surrounding region, there are several museums and cultural centers that will enrich your experience.

- **Zell am See Museum**: Located in the heart of the town, the Zell am See Museum offers a fascinating collection of local artifacts, showcasing the town's history from the Stone Age to the modern era. The museum's exhibits range from ancient archaeological finds to more contemporary pieces, including art and craftwork that reflect the local culture. If you're keen on learning more about the region's history, a visit here is a must.

- **Tauern Power Station (Kraftwerk Tauern)**: For a unique, off-the-beaten-path experience, head to the Tauern Power Station, one of the region's key hydroelectric plants. You can take a guided tour of the facility and learn about its role in powering the surrounding area while gaining insight into renewable energy practices in Austria.

The tours are informative and give visitors a chance to appreciate the region's modern contributions to sustainability.

- **Kitzsteinhorn Alpine Center**: Situated near Kaprun, this cultural center is dedicated to showcasing the natural wonders of the Kitzsteinhorn Glacier. The center offers educational exhibits about glacial ecology, alpine flora and fauna, and the history of the region's mountaineering culture. It's a great place to get a deeper understanding of the alpine environment before you venture out into the mountains.

Local Tip: If you're visiting Zell am See during the colder months, some museums might be closed, so check ahead and consider visiting during shoulder seasons when most attractions are open.

5.3 Natural Wonders (Beaches, Mountains, Lakes, National Parks)

The natural beauty of Zell am See is perhaps its most enchanting feature, with towering mountains, pristine lakes, and lush forests providing an outdoor playground for visitors. Whether you're an avid hiker or just looking to take in the scenery, the area offers something for everyone.

- **Lake Zell**: The jewel of Zell am See, Lake Zell is a stunning, crystal-clear freshwater lake that reflects the surrounding mountains like a mirror. It's a paradise for outdoor lovers, offering a wide range of activities. In the summer, you can swim, sail, or take a leisurely boat ride on the lake, while in winter, the shores of the lake turn into a serene winter wonderland. There are also plenty of walking and cycling paths around the lake, offering you a chance to soak in the spectacular scenery at a leisurely pace.

- **Schmittenhöhe**: For spectacular panoramic views, a hike or cable car ride to the summit of Schmittenhöhe is essential. Standing at 1,965 meters (6,447 feet), this mountain offers sweeping vistas of Zell am See, the surrounding valleys, and the distant peaks of the Alps. Whether you're skiing in the winter or hiking in the summer, the Schmittenhöhe offers an unforgettable experience in all seasons.

- Kitzsteinhorn Glacier: Accessible year-round, Kitzsteinhorn Glacier is an awe-inspiring natural wonder. Known as the "Glacier of Freedom," this towering ice field is a paradise for winter sports enthusiasts and those wanting to experience the beauty of the Austrian Alps in their purest form.

In the summer months, the glacier is also a popular hiking destination, and you can visit the Gipfelwelt 3000 viewing platform for unrivaled views of the surrounding peaks.

- **Hohe Tauern National Park**: Just a short drive from Zell am See, Hohe Tauern National Park is one of the largest nature reserves in Europe, home to diverse flora and fauna, including marmots, ibex, and golden eagles. With miles of hiking trails ranging from easy walks to more challenging alpine routes, the park is a hiker's dream. The park's pristine landscapes, dramatic waterfalls, and alpine meadows make it an essential stop for nature lovers.

Pro Tip: If you're visiting Zell am See in winter, make sure to dress warmly, as the alpine temperatures can be chilly even in the middle of the day, especially at higher altitudes.

5.4 Best Viewpoints & Photography Spots

Zell am See is a photographer's paradise, with its lakeside vistas, mountain backdrops, and charming town streets providing endless opportunities to capture stunning images. Whether you're a seasoned photographer or just want to snap a few memorable pictures, these spots are perfect for capturing the magic of this beautiful region.

- **Lake Zell from the Castle**: The view from Zell am See Castle offers one of the best perspectives of the town, the lake, and the surrounding mountains. The castle's hilltop location provides a sweeping panoramic view that captures the essence of the town's scenic beauty. It's especially striking at sunrise or sunset, when the colors of the sky reflect off the tranquil waters of Lake Zell.

- **Schmittenhöhe Summit**: From the top of Schmittenhöhe, the 360-degree views of the surrounding mountain ranges are jaw-dropping. The sight of the town of Zell am See sitting nestled between the lake and the towering Alps is truly one of the most iconic views in Austria. Whether you're hiking up or taking the cable car, be sure to bring your camera for some stunning shots.

- **Kitzsteinhorn Glacier**: For a truly dramatic landscape shot, head to the Gipfelwelt 3000 platform on the Kitzsteinhorn Glacier. With the surrounding peaks in sharp focus and the deep valleys below, it's a place where you can capture the power and majesty of the Austrian Alps in all their glory.

- **Zell am See Town Square**: For a quintessential shot of Zell am See, the Stadtplatz is your go-to spot. With its cobbled streets, colorful buildings, and the towering spire of St. Hippolyte's Church, it's the perfect scene for capturing the town's charm. Be sure to capture the reflections of the buildings in the clear waters of Lake Zell.

Photography Tip: Early morning or late afternoon are the best times for photos, as the lighting is softer and the crowds thinner, allowing you to capture the beauty of Zell am See without distractions.

Zell am See is a destination that enchants with its rich history, natural beauty, and diverse range of attractions. From the serene beauty of Lake Zell to the dramatic heights of the Kitzsteinhorn Glacier, this Alpine town offers a perfect mix of cultural, historical, and natural wonders. Whether you're capturing breathtaking photographs, exploring medieval castles, or simply soaking in the views, Zell am See will leave you with memories that will last a lifetime.

Chapter 6: Hidden Gems & Off-the-Beaten-Path Experiences

As much as Zell am See dazzles with its iconic landmarks and breathtaking vistas, the real magic of this Alpine town often lies in the quiet corners and lesser-known spots that most visitors overlook. It's in these places, tucked away from the bustling tourist routes, where you'll find the true heart of Zell am See authentic, unfiltered, and brimming with stories waiting to be discovered. In this chapter, I'll take you off the beaten path to the hidden gems and off-the-radar experiences that will give you a deeper, more intimate connection with this charming town.

6.1 Lesser-Known Attractions & Local Secrets

If you've already explored the main attractions of Zell am See, it's time to dig a little deeper and uncover the town's lesser-known treasures. These spots may not make every tourist brochure, but they offer some of the most authentic and enchanting experiences Zell am See has to offer.

- **Ruin Hohenwerfen Castle**: A 45-minute drive from Zell am See will take you to Hohenwerfen Castle, perched on a craggy rock above the Salzach Valley.

While it's not exactly hidden, it's often overshadowed by the more famous castles in the region. The medieval fortress dates back to the 11th century and offers a fantastic historical experience with its breathtaking views of the surrounding valleys. Unlike the tourist-heavy castles in the area, Hohenwerfen feels intimate and personal. The castle's falconry demonstrations are a highlight, giving you a glimpse into the ancient art of bird hunting in a stunning Alpine setting.

- **Glemmtaler Höhenweg**: For those looking to get away from the crowds, Glemmtaler Höhenweg is a hidden gem. This long-distance hiking trail, which spans over 100 kilometers, offers spectacular views of the Pinzgau and Salzach valleys, but it's far less trafficked than some of the more famous routes in the region. The trail is dotted with traditional mountain huts where you can enjoy a hearty meal while taking in the beauty of the Alps. The hike is perfect for those who want to experience Zell am See's natural wonders in a more peaceful, personal way.

- **Kapruner Ache Waterfall**: A short but invigorating walk from Kaprun leads you to the stunning Kapruner Ache Waterfall.

The power and beauty of the waterfall, framed by towering cliffs and dense greenery, will leave you awe-struck. While the waterfall is a bit of a local secret, those who do make the trek are rewarded with one of the most serene natural sites in the region. It's perfect for a quiet moment of reflection, and the surrounding forest provides a cool, shaded escape during the summer months.

Travel Tip: If you're venturing to these lesser-known spots, be sure to ask the locals for directions they're always happy to point you to the hidden gems of Zell am See that aren't in the guidebooks.

6.2 Underrated Neighborhoods & Villages

While Zell am See's town center is filled with charm, the true character of this region comes alive in its surrounding neighborhoods and villages, many of which remain off the radar for most tourists. These areas offer a slower, more authentic pace of life, and they're the perfect escape from the usual crowds.

- **Schüttdorf**: Just a few minutes from Zell am See's main square, Schüttdorf is a quiet village that often goes unnoticed by visitors. While it may not have the picturesque town square or the stunning views of Zell am See itself, Schüttdorf has its own unique charm. It's a perfect spot for those who prefer a more laid-back vibe.

The village is home to some wonderful traditional Alpine guesthouses and local cafés, offering the perfect opportunity to try some local pastries and freshly brewed coffee. For hikers, Schüttdorf is also a gateway to trails leading up to the Kitzsteinhorn Glacier.

- **Piesendorf**: A short drive from Zell am See, Piesendorf is a village that offers a glimpse of traditional rural life in the Austrian Alps. The charming village center is dotted with traditional wooden chalets, and the surrounding farms provide a picture-perfect backdrop of the region's agricultural beauty. Piesendorf is also home to several well-preserved churches and chapels that tell the story of the area's religious history. The village is a wonderful place to get off the beaten path and experience the simpler side of Austrian life.

- **Maishofen**: Nestled just north of Zell am See, Maishofen is another small village that has remained relatively untouched by mass tourism. Its location near the Saalach River means it offers beautiful riverside walks, and it's a great place to catch a glimpse of the region's local wildlife. In the winter, Maishofen transforms into a quiet, snow-covered village perfect for cross-country skiing and winter hikes.

The village is home to some exceptional, family-run restaurants that serve authentic Austrian dishes made from locally sourced ingredients.

Local Tip: These small villages are perfect for visitors who want to escape the tourist crowds and experience a more relaxed, authentic pace of life. Be sure to check out the local farmers' markets for fresh produce and handmade goods.

6.3 Unique Experiences Not Found in Typical Guides

When you've explored the usual tourist attractions and want to discover something truly unique, Zell am See offers experiences that you won't find in typical guidebooks. These are the kinds of adventures that will leave you with stories to tell and memories to cherish.

- **Night Skiing at Schmittenhöhe**: If you're visiting Zell am See in the winter, consider taking your skiing experience to the next level with night skiing at Schmittenhöhe. For a few select hours in the evening, the slopes of Schmittenhöhe are illuminated, offering a surreal experience of skiing under the stars. It's a magical way to see the mountain in a completely different light and one that's surprisingly peaceful compared to the daytime crowds.

Whether you're a seasoned skier or a novice, night skiing is an experience you won't forget.

- **E-bike Tours Around Lake Zell**: For a fun, eco-friendly way to explore the area, take an e-bike tour around Lake Zell. While walking around the lake offers its own beauty, cycling allows you to cover more ground and see the scenic viewpoints from a unique perspective. These guided e-bike tours are a perfect blend of adventure and relaxation as you glide past charming villages, pristine meadows, and stunning mountain backdrops. It's an ideal way to explore the area at your own pace, with a bit of extra help from the electric motor!

- **Zell am See Wine Tastings**: While Austria may not be the first country that comes to mind when you think of wine, Zell am See and the surrounding regions are home to some fantastic vineyards. Take part in a local wine-tasting experience, where you'll sample wines from the nearby Salzburgerland and Burgenland regions.

Whether you're sipping a crisp Grüner Veltliner or a rich Zweigelt, these tastings are a wonderful way to immerse yourself in local culture. Many wineries offer tours of their cellars, so you can learn about the winemaking process while enjoying some of the region's finest offerings.

Travel Tip: These unique experiences are often less crowded, so it's best to book in advance, especially if you're traveling during peak season.

Zell am See is a destination that offers more than meets the eye. Beyond the well-trodden tourist paths lies a wealth of hidden gems, off-the-beaten-path experiences, and local secrets that will make your trip truly special. Whether you're exploring medieval castles, relaxing in quiet villages, or indulging in a unique adventure, these hidden gems will give you a deeper connection to this stunning Alpine town. So, take the road less traveled, uncover these local treasures, and create your own unforgettable memories in Zell am See.

Chapter 7: Food & Drinks: A Culinary Journey

One of the true pleasures of traveling is indulging in a destination's culinary offerings, and Zell am See is no exception. The region's food scene is a rich tapestry of hearty alpine flavors, delicate mountain herbs, and fresh local ingredients, all tied to centuries-old traditions. Whether you're warming up after a day on the slopes, enjoying a lakeside sunset, or mingling with locals at a village café, Zell am See promises a delightful culinary journey. In this chapter, I'll guide you through the best traditional dishes, dining spots, and vibrant culinary experiences that will leave your taste buds begging for more.

7.1 Traditional Dishes to Try

No trip to Zell am See is complete without sampling its iconic Austrian dishes, each packed with history, flavor, and a true taste of the Alps.

- **Wiener Schnitzel**: The ultimate comfort food, the Wiener Schnitzel is a must-try dish when visiting Zell am See. This crispy, golden-brown, breaded veal cutlet is served with a side of potato salad or lingonberry jam.

While it's a dish you'll find across Austria, the version here is particularly satisfying crispy on the outside, tender on the inside, and oh-so-delicious.

- **Kaiserschmarrn**: If you have a sweet tooth, you can't miss Kaiserschmarrn, a fluffy shredded pancake served with warm plum compote or applesauce. Originally made as a royal treat for Emperor Franz Joseph, this dish is a beloved comfort food, perfect for sharing after a long day of sightseeing. The pancakes are light, sweet, and a delightful indulgence.

- **Tafelspitz**: For something a little more refined, try Tafelspitz, a traditional boiled beef dish served with horseradish, apple sauce, and a rich broth. This dish was once a royal favorite and is often enjoyed as a celebratory meal. It's an authentic taste of Austrian culinary tradition and an ideal choice for those who want to savor something truly local.

- **Pinzgauer Kasnocken**: A specialty from the Zell am See region, Pinzgauer Kasnocken are small dumplings made from fresh cheese and served with crispy onions and a rich, buttery sauce. They're the perfect side dish or vegetarian option, offering a taste of regional pride. The dumplings are soft, cheesy, and absolutely mouthwatering.

- **Salzburger Nockerl**: A light and fluffy meringue-based dessert, Salzburger Nockerl is a sweet end to any meal. The delicate soufflé is traditionally served with a dusting of powdered sugar and a dash of vanilla sauce. The contrast between the crisp outer shell and soft, creamy interior makes this dessert a delightful treat.

Local Tip: Make sure to ask your server for a recommendation when it comes to traditional local dishes. The chefs here take pride in serving the freshest seasonal ingredients, so the menu can change depending on what's in season.

7.2 Best Restaurants & Street Food Vendors

Zell am See's dining scene is varied, from fine dining restaurants with stunning lake views to humble family-run establishments that dish out the most delicious local fare. Whether you're after a fancy night out or a quick, tasty bite on the go, there's something for every palate.

- **Restaurant Kupferkessel**: Located right by the lake, Kupferkessel offers one of the most scenic dining experiences in Zell am See. The restaurant specializes in traditional Austrian dishes, with a focus on fresh fish from Lake Zell.

The ambiance is warm and inviting, and the views of the lake and mountains are unparalleled. Try their Zeller Forelle (trout from the lake), which is lightly smoked and served with seasonal vegetables.

- **Gasthof Fischerwirt**: This historic guesthouse and restaurant is a true local favorite, serving hearty alpine fare with an emphasis on regional ingredients. The cozy wooden interiors give it a homely feel, and the service is friendly and welcoming. Don't miss their Kasnocken (cheese dumplings) and Wiener Schnitzel, both of which are favorites among locals and tourists alike.

- **Seewirt Zauner**: If you're looking for an upscale dining experience, Seewirt Zauner is the place to go. This Michelin-recommended restaurant offers a modern twist on Austrian classics. The setting is elegant, with a gorgeous terrace overlooking Lake Zell. For a truly unforgettable dining experience, try their Tafelspitz, which is prepared with precision and paired with expertly selected wines.

- **Street Food Stalls at Zell am See's Main Square**: For a more casual meal, head to the main square of Zell am See, where street food vendors serve delicious quick bites, including bratwurst, sausages, pretzels, and potato-based snacks.

Grab a Bratwurst or a Käsekrainer (cheese-filled sausage) and enjoy it as you stroll through the charming streets.

- **The Wirtshaus Zum Hirschen**: Located in a quiet corner of the village, Zum Hirschen is perfect for a rustic, traditional Austrian meal. The restaurant's setting, complete with wooden beams and a crackling fireplace, creates a cozy atmosphere ideal for enjoying a hearty meal. Their Schnitzel and homemade desserts are fantastic, and the seasonal menu highlights the best of what the region has to offer.

Travel Tip: Make reservations for dinner, especially during the high season. Many of Zell am See's best restaurants fill up quickly due to their popularity among locals and tourists alike.

7.3 Cafés, Bars & Local Nightlife

When the sun sets over Lake Zell, the town transforms into a lively hub of cafés, bars, and nightlife. Whether you're looking to unwind with a coffee or enjoy a late-night cocktail, Zell am See has plenty to offer.

- **Café der Kunst**: This charming café is a great spot for a morning coffee or an afternoon tea. The interior is cozy and eclectic, with local artwork displayed on the walls.

The café's selection of cakes and pastries, especially their Apfelstrudel is to die for. It's the perfect place to sit and people-watch while sipping on a cup of freshly brewed Austrian coffee.

- **Bar 13**: For those looking to explore Zell am See's nightlife, Bar 13 is one of the best spots in town. Located near the lake, this trendy bar offers a stylish ambiance and an impressive list of cocktails. The bartenders are friendly and knowledgeable, happy to recommend something special based on your tastes. Whether you're in the mood for a classic cocktail or something more creative, you'll find it here.

- **Café Hirschenwirt**: This intimate café is known for its excellent coffee and fantastic selection of local cakes and pastries. It's a lovely spot to relax during the day, and the cozy interior makes it feel like a second home. In the evening, the café transforms into a cozy bar, offering drinks and cocktails with a side of great conversation.

- **Pension St. Georg Lounge Bar**: If you're looking for a more relaxed, upscale spot, head to the Pension St. Georg Lounge Bar. The bar has a warm, inviting atmosphere with a fireplace and plush seating.

They offer a range of expertly crafted cocktails and an extensive wine list, perfect for a sophisticated evening out.

7.4 Food Markets & Culinary Tours

For those who truly want to dive deep into the flavors of Zell am See, local food markets and culinary tours offer the perfect opportunity to sample regional delicacies and learn about the area's agricultural heritage.

- **Zell am See Farmer's Market**: Held every Saturday morning, the Zell am See Farmer's Market is a vibrant, bustling market where you can find fresh, locally grown produce, handmade cheeses, meats, and traditional Austrian baked goods. It's a fantastic place to pick up ingredients for a picnic or simply enjoy the lively atmosphere.

- **Pinzgauer Gourmet Tour**: For a unique experience, consider taking a Pinzgauer Gourmet Tour. This guided tour takes you through the best of Zell am See's culinary offerings, with stops at local farms, cheese dairies, and vineyards. Along the way, you'll get a firsthand look at how traditional Austrian products are made, and of course, you'll sample plenty of delicious food and drink.

Local Tip: If you're visiting during the holiday season, don't miss the Christmas markets in Zell am See, where you'll find local crafts, foods, and seasonal treats like Lebkuchen (gingerbread cookies) and mulled wine.

The culinary scene in Zell am See is a true reflection of the region's rich history, diverse landscapes, and love for fresh, local ingredients. Whether you're sitting down for a traditional Wiener Schnitzel, sipping a cocktail by the lake, or enjoying a lively farmer's market, every bite and every sip tells a story. So, come hungry and ready to explore the diverse flavors that make Zell am See a truly unforgettable destination. And as you do, be sure to savor each meal because in Zell am See, food is not just fuel; it's a journey in itself.

Chapter 8: Shopping & Souvenirs

Zell am See is not only a paradise for nature lovers and adventurers but also a treasure trove for those seeking unique shopping experiences. Whether you're searching for a chic boutique in the town center or looking to bring home a piece of Austrian craftsmanship, the area offers something for every shopper. In this chapter, I'll take you through the best shopping spots, where to find locally made goods, and the fine art of choosing the perfect souvenir to remember your time in this Alpine gem.

8.1 Best Shopping Districts & Malls

While Zell am See may not boast large-scale shopping malls like those found in major cities, the town's charm lies in its quaint, pedestrian-friendly streets and its blend of local shops, artisan boutiques, and charming stores tucked into the historic town center.

- **The Main Street (Hinterglemmstraße)**: This lively street is the heart of Zell am See's shopping scene. Stroll along this picturesque thoroughfare, where you'll find an eclectic mix of shops offering everything from Austrian fashion to home décor. The atmosphere is laid-back, and many of the stores are family-owned, adding to the sense of authenticity.

Be sure to pop into local clothing boutiques for stylish alpine wear or stop by the specialty stores for unique gifts and keepsakes.

- **The Zell am See Market Square (Rathausplatz)**: At the center of town, the Rathausplatz (Market Square) is not just a place to gather, but also a shopping hotspot. Surrounded by cozy cafés and historic buildings, this area is home to several shops selling high-quality souvenirs, local crafts, and Austrian delicacies like chocolate and cheese. You'll also find artisan shops that showcase handmade jewelry and local pottery, perfect for those looking for a special memento.

- **Schmittenhöhe Shopping Street**: For a unique shopping experience, take the gondola up to the Schmittenhöhe mountain. At the top, you'll find a small shopping area offering high-end outdoor gear, mountain apparel, and souvenirs that celebrate the surrounding natural beauty. The views from the top make this a shopping trip that's as much about the scenery as it is about the goods.

- **Zell am See's Outdoor Markets**: During the warmer months, outdoor markets are a common sight in Zell am See, offering everything from fresh produce to handcrafted goods.

These markets, such as the Farmers' Market on Saturdays, give you a chance to support local artisans and take home a piece of the region's agricultural bounty. From freshly baked goods to wooden carvings, there's something magical about shopping in an open-air market in the shadow of the Alps.

Local Tip: If you're planning to visit in the summer, the weekly markets in Zell am See are an unmissable experience. You'll find local farmers selling fresh berries, cheeses, and honey, all of which make excellent gifts.

8.2 Local Handicrafts, Art & Artisanal Goods

Zell am See is home to many talented artisans who create handmade goods that reflect the region's rich cultural heritage. If you're looking for a souvenir with a personal touch, there are plenty of options to choose from. The key here is to look beyond the mass-produced trinkets and focus on items that showcase the craftsmanship and spirit of the region.

- **Handcrafted Wooden Goods**: The Alps are renowned for their woodwork, and Zell am See is no exception. From finely carved figurines to rustic wooden kitchenware, these items make for a unique and lasting souvenir.

You'll find beautifully crafted wooden chalets, cooking utensils, or ornaments that are perfect reminders of your time in the region. Many local stores in the historic center sell these pieces, often made from locally sourced wood, like pine and spruce.

- **Pinzgauer Pottery**: One of the true gems of the region is Pinzgauer pottery, a traditional form of ceramic art that has been passed down through generations. The designs are often rustic and colorful, reflecting the stunning landscapes of the Pinzgau region. You can find everything from hand-painted mugs and plates to decorative vases. These are not just souvenirs they're pieces of art that hold the spirit of the Austrian Alps.

- **Austrian Textiles**: Zell am See is also known for its textiles, particularly woolen items like blankets, scarves, and socks. Local shops offer beautiful handwoven woolen products that are perfect for chilly evenings or as stylish additions to your wardrobe. The quality of the wool here is exceptional, making these items both practical and beautiful.

- **Austrian Jewelry**: Austrian jewelry designers create elegant, nature-inspired pieces that reflect the alpine landscape.

Look for delicate silver necklaces featuring mountain motifs or bracelets adorned with local gemstones, like the sparkling Austrian Crystal. These pieces make for timeless keepsakes or thoughtful gifts for loved ones.

- **Local Art**: For art enthusiasts, Zell am See offers several galleries featuring works from local painters and photographers. Many pieces focus on the stunning scenery, capturing the rugged mountains and serene lakes in a way that only an artist with a deep connection to the land can. These works are perfect for anyone looking to bring home a piece of the landscape, literally.

Local Tip: If you're visiting during the winter months, you may find additional artisanal products related to skiing and winter sports such as hand-knit hats, gloves, and warm woolen socks, perfect for your time on the slopes.

8.3 Budget-Friendly Shopping vs. Luxury Boutiques

No matter your budget, Zell am See offers an array of shopping options. Whether you're on the lookout for high-end designer goods or hoping to find a bargain that speaks to your journey, there's something for everyone.

- **Budget-Friendly Shopping**: If you're looking for souvenirs or gifts without breaking the bank, there are plenty of affordable options in Zell am See. The town's many specialty shops offer a range of reasonably priced items such as locally made chocolates, jams, and handmade scarves.

  The outdoor markets and local grocery stores also provide an excellent selection of locally produced goods, such as cheeses, sausages, and wines, all at very reasonable prices. For the budget-conscious traveler, these markets are perfect for picking up small gifts or treats to take home.

- **Affordable Fashion**: There are also several boutiques in the town center that sell stylish, high-quality Austrian fashion at affordable prices. From cozy knitwear to stylish outerwear, you'll find items that are both functional for the alpine climate and chic enough to wear on a night out. Many shops also offer sales and discounts, so if you're visiting during the off-season, you may be able to snag a deal on top-notch clothing.

- **Luxury Shopping**: For those looking to indulge, Zell am See has several high-end boutiques, especially around the lakeside areas and the Schmittenhöhe Shopping Street.

Designer labels like Loewe and BOSS have small but exclusive stores here, and if you're in search of a luxurious watch or piece of jewelry, the town's upscale boutiques are ready to cater to your desires. The mountain resorts around Zell am See are also home to luxury outlets that cater to the most discerning shoppers, offering top-of-the-line ski gear, fashion, and accessories.

- **Fine Wines & Spirits**: Zell am See is situated in a region renowned for its wine production. If you're looking for something special to take home, head to a wine shop or local delicatessen to pick up a bottle of Pinzgau wine or some local schnapps. These wines are often made from grapes grown in the foothills of the Alps, giving them a unique taste that you won't find elsewhere. Schnapps, an Austrian staple, comes in a variety of flavors, and it's a great way to bring a taste of Austria back home with you.

Travel Tip: Keep an eye out for seasonal sales or end-of-season discounts, particularly in winter and summer. Many stores will offer discounts during these times, so it's a great opportunity to grab designer items at a fraction of the cost.

Shopping in Zell am See is an experience that reflects the soul of the region timeless, authentic, and deeply connected to the natural world.

Whether you're wandering through quaint artisan shops, visiting local markets, or indulging in high-end boutiques, each item has a story to tell. From the intricate wooden carvings to the delicate Austrian crystal jewelry, Zell am See offers an array of treasures that are bound to bring a piece of the Alps home with you. So, take your time, explore the charming streets, and bring back a lasting memory of this beautiful alpine town.

Chapter 9: Outdoor Adventures & Activities

Zell am See is a paradise for outdoor enthusiasts. Nestled between the crystal-clear waters of Lake Zell and the majestic peaks of the Alps, this picturesque town offers an array of thrilling activities for every adventurer. Whether you're looking to explore the stunning alpine terrain on foot, glide across the water, or get your heart racing with some extreme sports, Zell am See has it all. Let me take you through the best outdoor adventures and activities, where each step and each moment will leave you with lasting memories of the natural beauty and adrenaline-pumping excitement that this alpine jewel has to offer.

9.1 Hiking, Biking, and Walking Tours

If there's one thing you must do in Zell am See, it's explore the surrounding landscapes. The region is a veritable hiking and biking paradise, with a variety of trails that cater to all levels of experience. Whether you're a seasoned hiker or someone who prefers a leisurely stroll, you'll find the perfect path.

- **Hiking Trails**: With the towering Schmittenhöhe mountain looming over the town and the serene shores of Lake Zell below, hiking here is nothing short of spectacular.

There are countless trails, ranging from easy lakeside walks to challenging mountain ascents. One of the most popular hikes is the Schmittenhöhe summit trail, which takes you to the top of the mountain, offering sweeping panoramic views of the town, lake, and the surrounding Alps. If you're looking for something a bit more relaxed, try the Zeller See Loop, a stunning 11 km trail that takes you around the lake, where you can stop for a picnic or simply sit and enjoy the views.

Local Tip: For those new to hiking, take the Zell am See-Kaprun Trail, a well-marked, easy-to-follow trail that gives you a great introduction to the area's stunning landscapes. The trail passes through lush forests, along babbling streams and offers breathtaking views of the surrounding peaks. Bring a packed lunch to enjoy at one of the many scenic resting points.

- **Biking Adventures**: Zell am See is an excellent destination for both road cyclists and mountain biking enthusiasts. The Tauern Cycle Path is one of the longest and most scenic cycling routes in Austria, stretching over 300 kilometers from the Salzburg region to Carinthia. But you don't have to commit to the entire route. You can easily bike part of it, taking in the beauty of the valley, forests, and the lake.

Mountain biking lovers will appreciate the challenging trails in the nearby Kitzsteinhorn Glacier area, where adrenaline-pumping descents and technical trails await.

Local Tip: Rent an e-bike if you want to explore the region without overexerting yourself. The gentle inclines along the lake or through the valley are made even more enjoyable with a little extra boost.

- **Guided Walking Tours**: For those who prefer to take a slower pace and immerse themselves in the region's rich history, guided walking tours are a fantastic option. A local guide will introduce you to the fascinating history of Zell am See, from its medieval roots to its development as a popular alpine destination. The walking tours often include hidden gems, tucked-away spots, and off-the-beaten-path locations that you might miss on your own.

9.2 Water Activities (Snorkeling, Diving, Boat Cruises)

While hiking and biking are certainly a big draw, Zell am See's location next to the sparkling waters of Lake Zell makes it a prime spot for water activities. Whether you want to paddle across the lake or dive into the depths, the options are abundant and unforgettable.

- **Boat Cruises**: The most relaxing way to take in the beauty of Lake Zell is aboard a boat cruise. I recommend hopping on one of the Zell am See boat tours, which offer a range of options, from short, scenic trips to longer excursions. As you cruise across the shimmering waters, you'll be treated to magnificent views of the surrounding mountains, charming villages, and the lush green forests that line the shores. On clear days, the reflection of the peaks on the water is simply mesmerizing.

Local Tip: The **Lake Zell sightseeing tour** is a must-do, as it covers all of the lake's scenic hotspots and provides fascinating insights into the area's history. Bring your camera this is one boat ride you'll want to remember!

- **Snorkeling & Diving**: While the lake may not be known for its coral reefs, the crystal-clear waters and underwater life make it a hidden gem for diving and snorkeling. There are several diving schools in the area where you can book a lesson or guided dive. The waters of Lake Zell are home to a variety of freshwater species, and if you're an experienced diver, you can explore deeper parts of the lake to discover hidden underwater landscapes.

Local Tip: If you're diving or snorkeling, bring a waterproof camera. The clarity of the water allows for fantastic underwater shots whether you're exploring the lake's flora or snapping pictures of the fish that swim past.

- **Water Sports**: For those seeking a bit of adventure on the water, Zell am See offers activities like wakeboarding, windsurfing, and stand-up paddleboarding (SUP). Renting equipment is easy, and you'll find several companies around the lake offering lessons for all levels. Paddleboarding, in particular, offers a peaceful way to enjoy the serenity of the lake while being surrounded by the towering peaks of the Alps.

9.3 Wildlife Experiences & Eco-Tourism

Zell am See's natural beauty isn't just for human enjoyment it's also home to a diverse range of wildlife. The region offers numerous opportunities to engage with nature, from observing local wildlife to participating in eco-friendly tours that highlight the region's environmental efforts.

- **Wildlife Watching**: If you're a nature lover, Zell am See offers the chance to see a variety of alpine wildlife.

You might spot red deer grazing on the slopes, marmots peeking from their burrows, or even the occasional golden eagle soaring high above the mountains. The Kitzsteinhorn Glacier area, in particular, is home to a range of protected species, including alpine ibex and chamois. If you're lucky, you might get a glimpse of these magnificent animals in their natural habitat.

- **Eco-Tourism**: Zell am See is committed to preserving its natural environment, and there are several eco-tourism initiatives that allow travelers to experience the region in an environmentally responsible way. Eco-friendly tours are available, where guides take you on a journey through the area's most pristine landscapes while educating you on local wildlife and conservation efforts. These tours typically focus on sustainable travel practices and include activities like nature walks, birdwatching, and forest exploration.

Local Tip: Check out the National Park Hohe Tauern, located just a short drive from Zell am See. It is Austria's largest national park and home to some of the country's most pristine wilderness areas. A guided tour here will take you deep into the heart of the Alps, offering an up-close look at the region's flora and fauna.

9.4 Extreme Sports & Adventure Activities

For adrenaline junkies, Zell am See is a playground of extreme sports. The surrounding mountains and lakes provide ample opportunities for thrill-seekers to push their limits and experience the Alps in a way most travelers can only dream of.

- **Paragliding**: Imagine soaring above Zell am See, the wind in your face, and the stunning landscape unfolding below you. Paragliding here is a once-in-a-lifetime experience, and the launch points from the Schmittenhöhe or Kitzsteinhorn Glacier offer some of the best aerial views you can get in the Alps. Tandem paragliding is popular for beginners, where a professional pilot will take you on a safe but thrilling ride over the town and surrounding mountains.

- **Canyoning**: If you're looking for an activity that combines adventure, nature, and water, canyoning is for you. This adrenaline-pumping sport involves rappelling down waterfalls, climbing through rocky gorges, and swimming through mountain streams. Several canyoning companies in the region offer guided tours, ensuring that you can experience this heart-racing activity in a safe and controlled environment.

- **Skiing & Snowboarding**: Zell am See is famous for its winter sports, and skiing and snowboarding here are second to none. With over 130 kilometers of ski slopes, the Zell am See-Kaprun ski area offers something for everyone. Whether you're a beginner or an advanced skier, the slopes of Schmittenhöhe and Kitzsteinhorn cater to all levels, and the stunning winter scenery is an added bonus.

Local Tip: The **Kitzsteinhorn Glacier** is open year-round for skiing, so if you're visiting in the summer, you can still enjoy skiing on the glacier.

Whether you're hiking to a summit for panoramic views, gliding across Lake Zell's glassy waters, encountering local wildlife, or indulging in extreme sports that get your heart racing, Zell am See offers an unforgettable outdoor adventure for every kind of traveler. The beauty of this alpine paradise is that it caters to all levels of adventurers, from those seeking peaceful nature walks to those hungry for adrenaline. So, pack your gear, lace up your boots, and dive into the outdoor experiences that make Zell am See one of the most exciting destinations in Austria.

Chapter 10: Cultural Experiences & Local Traditions

Zell am See is more than just a postcard-perfect destination of towering peaks and crystal-clear waters it's a vibrant tapestry of cultural heritage, age-old traditions, and artistic expressions. As you step off the beaten path and immerse yourself in the town's rich cultural scene, you'll discover the essence of its people, their stories, and the customs they hold dear. This chapter will guide you through the most captivating cultural experiences that will enhance your trip, allowing you to connect with Zell am See on a deeper level.

10.1 Understanding Local Customs & Etiquette

Austria is renowned for its warm hospitality, and Zell am See, a town nestled within the heart of the Salzburgerland region, is no exception. As you stroll through the charming streets and interact with locals, it's helpful to understand the social norms that shape daily life here. Familiarizing yourself with a few key customs and etiquette will enrich your travel experience and help you engage with the people you meet.

- **Politeness is Key**: Austrians are known for their politeness and formal manners, especially when meeting new people.

When greeting someone, it's common to use "Guten Morgen" (Good morning) or "Grüß Gott" (God greet you) followed by a handshake. In more casual settings, such as with friends, "Hallo" or "Servus" (informal hello) are often used.

- **Table Etiquette**: Austrians take their dining experiences seriously. When you're invited to a meal, wait until everyone is seated before starting. When clinking glasses in a toast, make sure to make eye contact it's a tradition symbolizing respect. Don't forget to say "Prost!" (Cheers) before you take a sip. And if you're enjoying a typical Austrian meal, expect to be offered a dessert at the end of your meal. Austrians have a deep appreciation for their cakes and pastries.

- **Dress Code**: While Zell am See has a relaxed and welcoming atmosphere, dressing smartly is appreciated in many establishments, especially restaurants or cultural events. While in outdoor settings, such as hiking, casual attire is perfectly fine, when visiting churches or attending local concerts, it's considered respectful to dress a bit more formally.

- **Tipping**: Tipping is customary in Austria, and it's generally expected to leave a 5-10% tip in restaurants. For smaller purchases or services (e.g., at cafés or taxis), rounding up the bill is appreciated, though not mandatory.

Local Tip: While many Austrians speak English, learning a few basic German phrases will go a long way and show your respect for the culture. Even a simple "Danke" (Thank you) will be warmly appreciated.

10.2 Festivals & Traditional Celebrations

Zell am See, like many Austrian towns, is a place where tradition is celebrated with gusto. The cultural calendar is dotted with festivals and events that highlight the region's deep connection to its heritage, from alpine folklore to modern celebrations of art and music. Here are a few that you should try to experience during your visit:

- **Zeller Lake Festival**: This summer festival is one of the biggest events in the town, held along the banks of the scenic Lake Zell. The festival brings together the best of local culture, with live folk music, food stalls serving Austrian specialties, and traditional dances. The sight of the town illuminated at night against the backdrop of the lake is an unforgettable experience.

- **Alpine Folklore Festivals**: Austria's alpine culture runs deep, and no place showcases this better than Zell am See. Several times throughout the year, you can enjoy folk music performances, traditional dances, and displays of local craftsmanship. During these festivals, you'll see locals wearing their beautiful dirndls and lederhosen, two iconic symbols of Austrian folk attire.

- **Christmas Markets**: During the winter months, Zell am See transforms into a winter wonderland, and the Christmas markets are the highlight of the season. The town square is filled with wooden stalls selling handmade ornaments, candles, and traditional Austrian treats like Lebkuchen (gingerbread cookies) and Glühwein (mulled wine). It's the perfect time to experience the warmth of Austrian hospitality, wrapped in the festive glow of holiday lights.

- **Music Festivals**: Zell am See also has a rich musical heritage. The Zell am See Music Festival, held annually, brings together classical musicians from around the world. If you're a fan of music, attending a concert at one of the town's beautiful churches or in the open-air settings around the lake is an extraordinary cultural experience. Whether you prefer opera, symphonic concerts, or more contemporary genres, you'll find a rich diversity of performances to enjoy.

Local Tip: If you're visiting in winter, try to catch a traditional Austrian Advent concert an experience that combines the serene atmosphere of the holiday season with the beautiful sounds of local choirs and musicians.

10.3 Music, Dance, and Art Scene

The cultural scene in Zell am See is defined by its love of music, dance, and art. Whether you're drawn to the melodies of local orchestras or captivated by the artistry of the town's galleries, there's plenty here to explore.

- **Classical Music**: Zell am See is home to several world-class music institutions, and classical music is a central part of local life. The town regularly hosts classical music concerts, many of which are held in stunning settings like the St. Hippolyte Church or in the outdoor concert areas by the lake. The Konzertverein Zell am See is an important part of the town's musical scene, offering both orchestral performances and chamber music.

- **Traditional Dance**: Austrian folk dancing is another way locals celebrate their cultural heritage, and Zell am See is no exception. Traditional dance events are organized throughout the year, where you can watch or even join in.

If you're lucky enough to be here during a festival, don't miss the chance to see a Volksmusik concert, where dancers in traditional attire twirl and spin in perfect harmony with lively Austrian folk tunes.

- **Art and Galleries**: Zell am See is a town with a deep appreciation for the arts. While exploring, you'll come across several small galleries that showcase local and regional artists. From stunning landscapes that capture the beauty of the Alps to contemporary pieces, the art scene here offers something for every taste. Be sure to check out the Kunsthaus Salden for rotating exhibitions and an insight into local artistic expression.

Local Tip: If you're in the mood for something truly local, head to the Zell am See Art Walk, a self-guided tour through various galleries that celebrate both historical and modern artists from the region.

10.4 Historical Influences on the Culture

Zell am See's culture has been shaped by centuries of history, from Roman times to its more recent transformation into a resort town. As you walk through the cobblestone streets and explore the town's architecture, you'll be stepping through layers of history that have influenced the local traditions and customs.

- **Roman and Medieval Influence**: The area around Zell am See has been inhabited since Roman times, and the remnants of this ancient culture are still present today. One of the most prominent historical sites is the Stadtplatz, where you'll find charming medieval architecture mixed with more modern buildings. The town's Kaprun Castle, located just outside Zell am See, was originally built in the 12th century and offers a glimpse into the area's feudal past.

- **Alpine Traditions**: The region's alpine traditions, including yodeling, cheese-making, and mountain farming, have been passed down through generations. Zell am See's farmers and craftsmen are the keepers of these traditions, and you can experience them firsthand by visiting local farms or enjoying the hand-made goods in the town's shops. The Kitzsteinhorn Glacier is a testament to the area's rugged mountain history and has become a symbol of local pride.

- **Tourism and the Modern Age**: In the late 19th and early 20th centuries, Zell am See began to transform into a popular tourist destination, attracting visitors from all over the world with its stunning landscapes and winter sports. This influx of travelers helped shape the town into the vibrant, cosmopolitan place it is today while still retaining its deep connection to local traditions.

Local Tip: Make sure to stop by the Zell am See Museum, where you can learn more about the town's fascinating history, including its Roman roots and its evolution into a popular alpine resort.

Zell am See is a place where culture, tradition, and history blend seamlessly with breathtaking landscapes. Whether you're participating in local festivals, enjoying a performance at a classical concert, or simply admiring the town's rich artistic heritage, the cultural experiences here are as captivating as the surroundings themselves. Immerse yourself in the region's customs and traditions, and you'll leave with a deeper understanding and appreciation for the people who call this alpine paradise home.

Chapter 11: Seasonal Travel Guide

The charm of Zell am See is ever-changing, and every season offers a unique opportunity to explore this stunning Alpine paradise. Whether you're drawn to the vibrant green landscapes of spring, the sun-drenched adventures of summer, the rich colors of autumn, or the winter wonderland blanketed in snow, Zell am See's seasonal beauty makes it an irresistible year-round destination. In this chapter, I'll guide you through the highlights of each season, offering tips on what to expect, what to do, and how to make the most of your trip at any time of the year.

11.1 Visiting in Spring (March – May)

Spring in Zell am See is like a gentle awakening, where the snow begins to melt, the days grow longer, and nature begins to reassert its vibrant colors. The town is still quite peaceful compared to the summer rush, making it a fantastic time for those who enjoy a slower pace but still want to experience all that the area has to offer.

- **A Burst of Color**: As the snow recedes from the meadows, the landscape is painted with wildflowers and fresh greenery. The sight of the snow-capped mountains with the first signs of blooming flowers at their feet is nothing short of magical.

It's the perfect time to take long, leisurely walks around Lake Zell, where the crisp air and scenic beauty come together for an unforgettable experience.

- **Spring Skiing**: If you're visiting Zell am See in early spring, you can still catch the tail end of ski season, especially on the Kitzsteinhorn Glacier. This high-altitude resort ensures good snow conditions well into spring, allowing you to enjoy the slopes with fewer crowds. The spring sunshine and slightly warmer temperatures make skiing in the morning and enjoying a leisurely lunch in the sun afterward a perfect combination.

- **Hiking & Biking**: With the snow starting to melt, spring is an ideal time to explore Zell am See's hiking and biking trails. From easy lakeside walks to more challenging mountain hikes, the options are endless. The Schmittenhöhe mountain, which is accessible via a cable car, is a popular spot for early-season hiking, offering panoramic views of the town, the lake, and the surrounding Alps.

Local Tip: The spring months are less crowded, so it's a great time to book your accommodation at a fraction of the price compared to peak summer season.

- **Local Festivals**: Spring brings with it a number of smaller, more intimate festivals, where you can get a taste of Austrian folk music, local food, and culture. The Alpine Spring Festival, for example, celebrates the arrival of the warmer weather with music, dancing, and traditional Austrian cuisine.

11.2 Summer Adventures (June – August)

Summer in Zell am See is when the town truly comes to life. The weather is warm, the sun is out, and the town and its surroundings offer an incredible array of activities for all kinds of travelers. It's the high season, meaning more visitors, but it also means that everything you want to do is available, from outdoor adventures to cultural experiences.

- **Water Sports on Lake Zell**: One of the highlights of summer in Zell am See is the opportunity to enjoy the crystal-clear waters of Lake Zell. The lake is perfect for a variety of water activities, including swimming, windsurfing, sailing, and stand-up paddleboarding. There are rental shops along the lakefront where you can gear up and spend hours enjoying the water.

- **Hiking & Adventure in the Alps**: The trails around Zell am See are some of the best for hiking, trekking, and mountain biking in the summer. If you're up for a challenge, hike to the summit of Schmittenhöhe for jaw-dropping views or take a more leisurely stroll through the lush forests and alpine meadows. Biking enthusiasts can also take advantage of the well-maintained biking routes that wind their way through the valley and up into the mountains.

- **Festivals & Events**: Summer is when Zell am See is at its most festive, with numerous events taking place throughout the season. The Zeller See Fest is one of the biggest celebrations, with live music, dancing, and food stalls along the lakeside. In addition, open-air concerts and cultural performances are frequent, and if you're here in July or August, you'll likely be able to catch a performance by the Zell am See Music Festival, where talented musicians from around the world perform in picturesque venues.

- **Relaxing on the Lakeside**: If adventure isn't on your itinerary, the summer months are ideal for simply relaxing by the lake. There are several beautiful beaches and swimming areas around Lake Zell, where you can soak up the sun, swim in the clear waters, and enjoy a laid-back day.

Local Tip: The summer months can be busy, so it's advisable to book your accommodation early, especially if you're planning to stay near the lake or in the town center.

11.3 Autumn Charm (September – November)

Autumn in Zell am See is a season of transformation. The vibrant fall colors paint the landscape in shades of gold, red, and amber, and the cool, crisp air brings a sense of tranquility to the town. This is a quieter time of year, offering the chance to experience the town and surrounding areas in a more peaceful, reflective setting.

- **Foliage Hikes & Scenic Drives**: The mountains and forests around Zell am See are stunning during autumn, with the changing leaves providing a beautiful backdrop for hikes and walks. The Glocknerstraße, one of Austria's most scenic routes, winds through the Hohe Tauern National Park and is particularly breathtaking during the fall, offering spectacular views of the snow-capped peaks juxtaposed against the fiery colors of the forest below. The Schmittenhöhe also offers autumn hiking routes with views that seem to stretch for miles.

- **Wine & Culinary Delights**: Autumn is also harvest time in the region, and Zell am See celebrates this with a variety of food and wine festivals.

Sample locally produced wines from the Salzburgerland wine region, paired with hearty Austrian dishes such as Tafelspitz (boiled beef with horseradish) or Apfelstrudel (apple strudel). Many local restaurants and markets offer seasonal specialties during this time, so it's an excellent opportunity to savor fresh, regional flavors.

- **Peaceful Vibes**: With fewer tourists, autumn in Zell am See has a relaxed, almost intimate feel. The crowds of summer have dissipated, leaving the town quiet enough for you to explore at your own pace. If you're looking for a slower, more reflective experience, this is the perfect time to visit.

Local Tip: The weather in autumn can be unpredictable, so be sure to pack layers and be prepared for occasional rain showers, especially in October.

11.4 Winter Wonderland (December – February)

Winter in Zell am See is a magical time, when the town transforms into a snowy paradise, attracting visitors from around the world for its world-class skiing, cozy alpine atmosphere, and festive charm. The winter months are the most popular for those seeking outdoor winter adventures, but they also offer a perfect setting for those looking for peace and relaxation by the fireside.

- **Skiing & Snowboarding**: Zell am See is a premier destination for skiing and snowboarding. With a vast ski area that includes Schmittenhöhe and the Kitzsteinhorn Glacier, you'll find excellent slopes for all levels. The high-altitude glacier ensures skiing well into the spring months, while the Schmittenhöhe offers a great range of runs for beginners and intermediates.

- **Winter Hiking & Snowshoeing**: If you're not a skier, there are plenty of other winter activities to enjoy. Winter hiking is a favorite pastime, with well-marked trails that take you through snow-covered forests and around the lake. Snowshoeing is also popular and offers a more serene way to explore the landscape at a slow pace.

- **Christmas Markets & Festivities**: Zell am See's Christmas markets are a highlight of the winter season, with twinkling lights, festive music, and stalls selling handcrafted ornaments, hot drinks, and delicious pastries. The Zell am See Christmas Market in the town square is the perfect place to get into the holiday spirit, where you can warm up with a cup of Glühwein and shop for unique, local gifts.

- **Cozy Winter Vibes**: After a day of outdoor adventures, nothing beats warming up in a cozy café or local restaurant.

Try traditional Austrian Kaiserschmarrn (shredded pancakes) or sip hot chocolate while gazing at the snow outside. The town's alpine chalets and hotels provide the perfect setting to unwind and enjoy the serenity of winter.

Local Tip: Winter can be busy, especially around Christmas and New Year's, so book your accommodations well in advance to secure the best spots.

No matter when you decide to visit Zell am See, each season offers a fresh perspective on this breathtaking town. From the springtime renewal of nature to the full-throttle summer adventures, the colorful fall foliage, and the winter wonderland that turns the region into a snow-covered playground, Zell am See is a destination that will leave you with lasting memories. So, pack your bags and get ready to explore each season promises a new and unforgettable experience.

Chapter 12: Itineraries for Every Type of Traveler

Zell am See is a town that can cater to every kind of traveler, whether you have only a day to explore or an entire week to immerse yourself in its beauty. The magic of this alpine gem is that it offers something for everyone, from the thrill-seeker to the peace-seeker, from families to couples, and everyone in between. In this chapter, I'll guide you through a range of thoughtfully curated itineraries that will help you make the most of your time in Zell am See, no matter your interests or the length of your stay.

12.1 24-Hour Express Itinerary

If you've only got one day to experience Zell am See, don't worry you can still see the highlights and get a taste of its charm. Here's how to make every minute count:

- **Morning**: Start your day with a peaceful stroll along Lake Zell, taking in the serene views of the water and surrounding mountains. Grab a coffee from one of the lakeside cafes and take in the tranquility of the morning. Then, head up the Schmittenhöhe mountain via the cable car for panoramic views of the town and the entire valley.

Even if you're not an avid hiker, the views from the top will make your trip worth it. The alpine air and sweeping vistas are the perfect introduction to Zell am See.

- **Lunch**: Descend back into town for lunch at a traditional Austrian restaurant, like Restaurant Seevilla. Try a classic Wiener Schnitzel or Kaiserschmarrn, the famous shredded pancakes, to fuel up for your next adventure.

- **Afternoon**: Head to the Zell am See Old Town, where you can wander through the cobblestone streets, visit St. Hippolytus Church, and explore the quaint shops and boutiques. If you're a history buff, make sure to check out the Zell am See Museum for a deeper dive into the area's rich heritage.

- **Evening**: For your last few hours, take a sunset boat tour on Lake Zell. The gentle ripples of the water as the sun sets behind the mountains create a perfect, tranquil finish to your day. End with a cozy dinner at a lakeside restaurant, such as Bräuhaus Zell am See, for a local beer and hearty fare.

12.2 3-Day Classic Itinerary

A three-day itinerary allows you to dig a little deeper into Zell am See's wonders and also explore its surrounding areas.

Day 1: Exploration and Scenic Views

- **Morning**: Start your day with a visit to Schmittenhöhe for breathtaking views of the Alps. You can hike, but if you're short on time, take the cable car to the summit. From there, spend some time at the Kitzsteinhorn Glacier if you're looking to add some snow to your adventure, even in summer.

- **Afternoon**: After lunch in the town center, spend the afternoon on Lake Zell. Whether you want to take a boat ride, go paddleboarding, or just relax by the shore, the lake is central to the Zell am See experience.

- **Evening**: Enjoy a leisurely dinner at a traditional Austrian restaurant like Kupferkessel, where the rustic setting and local dishes will immerse you in the region's culinary delights.

Day 2: Hiking and Culture

- **Morning**: After a hearty breakfast, head to the Glocknerstraße, one of Austria's most scenic drives, for an unforgettable journey through the mountains. Stop along the way for photo ops and short hikes, like the one leading to the Pasterze Glacier.

- **Afternoon**: Return to Zell am See for lunch, then visit the Zell am See Museum to learn about the area's history, from its Roman past to the modern-day ski resort. Afterwards, enjoy a walking tour through the town's medieval streets, where you can explore charming shops and cafes.

- **Evening**: For dinner, head to Alpenstern for a fine dining experience with panoramic views of the lake and mountains.

Day 3: Adventure and Relaxation

- **Morning**: Begin your day with a more adventurous activity like mountain biking or hiking along the Pinzgauer Spaziergang trail, which offers spectacular views and a bit of a challenge.

- **Afternoon**: After a satisfying lunch, treat yourself to a relaxing afternoon at a wellness spa, such as the Tauern Spa, where you can soak in the thermal pools while enjoying views of the mountains.

- **Evening**: For your final night, enjoy a gourmet dinner at Zeller Seefest restaurant, where the lake views and excellent food provide the perfect farewell to your trip.

12.3 7-Day In-Depth Itinerary

For those who have the luxury of a week to explore Zell am See, a seven-day itinerary allows you to dive into both the local culture and natural beauty in depth.

Day 1-2: Lake Zell and Surroundings

- Spend your first two days exploring the lake, taking a boat tour, and spending time at Schmittenhöhe and Kitzsteinhorn. Visit the nearby Kaprun area, with its glacier ski resorts and hiking paths. If you're into winter sports, this is the time to enjoy early season skiing.

- For a relaxing evening, visit the Zell am See Old Town, enjoy local coffee shops, and try a different restaurant each night to sample various regional delicacies.

Day 3-4: Hiking, Biking, and Outdoor Adventures

- On day three, set out for a full day of hiking or mountain biking. The Glocknerstraße offers incredible mountain views, while the Schmittenhöhe hiking trails provide both easy and moderate hikes.

- For something more leisurely, consider a cycling trip along Lake Zell, where the gentle slopes make for a relaxing and scenic ride.

Day 5: Culture & History

- Dedicate a day to exploring the historical side of Zell am See. Visit the Zell am See Museum and St. Hippolytus Church, followed by a walking tour of the old town. If you're a fan of Austrian history, the Kaprun Castle is another fascinating historical site to explore.

Day 6: Day Trips to Surrounding Villages

- Take a day trip to nearby villages like Lend or Piesendorf, where you can experience authentic rural Austria and visit local farmers' markets or enjoy a quiet café by the river.

Day 7: Relaxation and Pampering

- End your trip with a day of relaxation at the Tauern Spa. Enjoy a massage, a dip in the thermal pools, and unwind with panoramic views of the mountains and valley.

12.4 Family-Friendly Itinerary

Zell am See is an excellent destination for families with children, offering both adventure and relaxation in equal measure. Here's how to create the perfect family itinerary.

Day 1: Arrival and Exploration

- Take the family for a leisurely walk around Lake Zell, where kids can enjoy the playgrounds along the lake and parents can relax by the water. Consider renting bikes for a family cycling trip around the lake.

Day 2: Skiing or Snow Fun

- If you're visiting in the winter, spend the day skiing at Schmittenhöhe or Kitzsteinhorn, both of which have excellent facilities for families. There are beginner slopes for kids and excellent ski schools for first-timers.

- If it's summer, explore the Schmittenhöhe for gentle hiking trails that are family-friendly and full of scenic views.

Day 3: Outdoor Adventure and Relaxation

- After a morning of adventure, treat your family to a relaxing afternoon at the Tauern Spa, which offers child-friendly areas like the outdoor water park.

12.5 Romantic Getaway for Couples

Zell am See is a dream destination for couples seeking romance, with its stunning alpine scenery, tranquil lake, and intimate atmosphere.

Day 1: A Romantic Stroll by the Lake

- Start with a lakeside stroll, followed by a romantic dinner at Bräuhaus Zell am See, where you can enjoy Austrian specialties in a cozy setting.

Day 2: Adventure Together

- Hike to Schmittenhöhe for incredible views and a peaceful, secluded moment. If you're feeling adventurous, take a boat ride on Lake Zell.

Day 3: Spa Day and Wine Tasting

- Treat yourselves to a day at the Tauern Spa, then spend the evening enjoying a wine tasting in a nearby vineyard.

12.6 Budget Traveler's Itinerary

Zell am See can be surprisingly affordable, even for budget-conscious travelers. Here's how to experience the best of the area on a budget.

Day 1: Explore the Outdoors

- Take advantage of free activities like hiking, cycling, and strolling around Lake Zell. You can enjoy the beautiful surroundings without spending much money.

Day 2: Visit Museums and Local Markets

- Spend the day exploring the Zell am See Museum and the local markets. Many of the town's attractions have a minimal entry fee, allowing you to experience the history of the area without breaking the bank.

Day 3: Outdoor Fun

- Take a day trip to Kaprun for some hiking or free sightseeing at Kaprun Castle and the Kaprun Reservoirs. These are all free or have a very small fee.

12.7 Luxury & VIP Experience Itinerary

If you're looking for a lavish Alpine retreat, this itinerary will cater to your every indulgence.

- Stay at Grand Hotel Zell am See, a five-star lakeside resort.
- Dine at Salzburgerstube, known for gourmet dining with Alpine flair.
- Exclusive activities: Helicopter tours, private yacht cruises, and spa treatments.

No matter what type of traveler you are, Zell am See offers an unforgettable experience tailored just for you.

Whether you're here for a short visit or an extended stay, there's an itinerary that will help you discover the very best of this Austrian gem. So, pack your bags, plan your adventure, and get ready to explore the stunning beauty of Zell am See!

Chapter 13: Day Trips & Nearby Excursions

Zell am See is a paradise in its own right, but there's something truly special about venturing beyond its borders to explore the surrounding areas. The regions around Zell am See are brimming with fascinating landscapes, charming towns, and unforgettable experiences. Whether you're interested in discovering nearby towns, embarking on scenic road trips, or indulging in coastal escapes, there's always something new to explore. In this chapter, I'll share some of the best day trips and excursions, so you can make the most of your time in the area.

13.1 Best Nearby Towns & Cities to Visit

If you're staying in Zell am See, you're perfectly positioned to explore some nearby towns and cities that are just as rich in culture, history, and natural beauty.

Kaprun: A Short Drive to the Mountains

A mere 15-minute drive from Zell am See, Kaprun is an absolute must-visit for nature lovers and thrill-seekers. While Zell am See is known for its lake, Kaprun is all about the mountains.

The town is famous for its Kitzsteinhorn Glacier, a year-round ski resort, and the Kaprun High Altitude Reservoirs, which offer awe-inspiring views. Even if you're not a skier, the scenic cable car ride to the glacier is well worth it. In the summer, the area transforms into a hiking and mountain biking haven.

- **What to do**: Explore the glaciers, hike to the reservoirs, visit the Kaprun Castle, or relax at the Tauern Spa, a luxurious spa offering panoramic views of the mountains.

- **Travel Tip**: The Zell am See-Kaprun Card offers discounts for many attractions, including the Kitzsteinhorn cable car and the Tauern Spa.

Lienz: Alpine Charm with Italian Influence

Located about two hours south of Zell am See, Lienz is a picturesque town in the Austrian Alps that boasts a unique blend of Austrian and Italian cultures. This charming town, with its narrow streets and colorful buildings, offers a slower pace of life, perfect for those seeking a relaxing escape. Visit the Burg Bruck Museum to learn about Lienz's history, or simply wander through the old town, soaking in the charming architecture and local cafés.

- **What to do**: Stroll through the old town, visit Burg Bruck Museum, or take a scenic drive up to Drau Valley for breathtaking alpine views.

- **Travel Tip**: Try some local Italian-Austrian fusion dishes, such as Tyrolean speck paired with a glass of Grüner Veltliner wine.

Salzburg: A Day of Culture and Music

Just under two hours from Zell am See, Salzburg is one of the most culturally rich cities in Austria. Known as the birthplace of Mozart and the setting for The Sound of Music, Salzburg offers a blend of baroque architecture, classical music, and stunning alpine scenery. Wander through Mirabell Gardens, visit Hohensalzburg Fortress, and stroll along the winding streets of the Altstadt (Old Town), a UNESCO World Heritage site.

- **What to do**: Visit Mozart's Birthplace, explore Hohensalzburg Fortress, and take a boat trip on the Salzach River.

- **Travel Tip**: If you're a fan of classical music, time your visit with one of the many summer music festivals in Salzburg, such as the Salzburg Festival.

13.2 Scenic Road Trips & Train Journeys

One of the most enjoyable ways to see the area around Zell am See is by hitting the road or hopping on a scenic train journey.

The landscapes surrounding the town are as stunning as they come, and there's no better way to experience them than through these unforgettable routes.

The Grossglockner High Alpine Road: A Breathtaking Journey

If you're a fan of dramatic mountain scenery, the Grossglockner High Alpine Road should be at the top of your list. This iconic road takes you through the Hohe Tauern National Park and offers some of the most breathtaking views of Austria's tallest mountain, Grossglockner. The route is open from May to October, and as you drive along the winding roads, you'll be treated to views of glaciers, alpine meadows, and towering peaks.

- **What to do**: Stop at the Franz-Josefs-Höhe lookout for a jaw-dropping view of the Grossglockner. Visit the Pasterze Glacier and take a short hike to see it up close.
- **Travel Tip**: The road can be busy during peak season, so try to start your trip early in the morning to avoid crowds.

The Zeller See Panoramic Road: A Short but Sweet Scenic Drive

For a shorter, yet equally stunning, road trip, take the Zeller See Panoramic Road. This scenic route encircles Lake Zell and offers incredible views of the lake, mountains, and surrounding villages. Whether you're enjoying a leisurely drive or cycling around the lake, this route will leave you mesmerized by its natural beauty.

- **What to do**: Stop at one of the charming lakeside cafés or beaches, take a boat tour of Lake Zell, or rent a bike to explore the area.

- **Travel Tip**: Don't forget your camera this road offers plenty of opportunities for stunning photos, especially at sunset.

The Pinzgau Railway: A Journey Through Alpine Villages

For train enthusiasts, the Pinzgau Railway is an absolute treat. This narrow-gauge railway travels through the Pinzgau Valley, offering passengers panoramic views of the surrounding mountains and valleys. Starting from Zell am See, the train journey winds through lush forests and picturesque villages, making it one of the most scenic train rides in Austria.

- **What to do**: Hop off at one of the charming villages along the way, like Mittersill or Hollersbach, and take in the peaceful atmosphere of rural Austria.

- **Travel Tip**: The train ride is especially magical in the winter when the entire valley is covered in snow, creating a fairytale-like landscape.

13.3 Island Hopping & Coastal Escapes

While Zell am See may be nestled in the Alps, the journey to the Austrian coastline, especially during the warmer months, offers an array of exciting day trips to nearby lakes, and coastal towns. Austria may not have a coastline, but its lakes and rivers provide a wealth of stunning, almost Mediterranean-like escapes.

Lake Wolfgang: Serenity and Stunning Views

Around an hour's drive from Zell am See, Lake Wolfgang (or Wolfgangsee) is another gorgeous lake surrounded by mountains, and it's perfect for a day of relaxation. The village of St. Wolfgang is particularly charming, with its cobblestone streets and historic buildings, including the Pilgrimage Church. The lake itself is perfect for boat tours, swimming, and fishing.

- **What to do**: Take a boat tour on the lake, hike up to Schafberg Mountain for panoramic views, or simply relax by the lake at one of the quaint lakeside cafés.
- **Travel Tip**: Try the famous St. Wolfgang's fish, served at several lakeside restaurants.

Lake Neusiedl: Austria's Largest Steppe Lake

For a more unique experience, head to Lake Neusiedl, located about 3 hours east of Zell am See, near the Hungarian border.

This UNESCO World Heritage-listed lake is famous for its wide, flat expanses of water, surrounded by vast reed beds and wine-growing regions. The area is great for birdwatching, and its surrounding towns are perfect for wine lovers who want to explore Austria's lesser-known wine regions.

- **What to do**: Rent a bike to cycle around the lake, visit the Seewinkel National Park, or take a boat trip.
- **Travel Tip**: Stop at one of the local wineries in Rust or Mörbisch to sample some of the region's excellent white wines.

The beauty of Zell am See is not only found in the town itself but also in its surroundings. Whether you're taking a scenic road trip, hopping on a train, or visiting nearby towns, the area offers a plethora of day trips and excursions that will enrich your travel experience. From the dramatic Grossglockner High Alpine Road to the serene shores of Lake Wolfgang, you'll discover new landscapes, cultures, and experiences that will stay with you long after you leave.

No matter what type of traveler you are, Zell am See's surroundings are sure to offer something unforgettable. So, pack your bags, hit the road, and start exploring!

Chapter 14: Nightlife & Entertainment

As the sun dips behind the mountains and the stars begin to twinkle over the serene waters of Lake Zell, the town of Zell am See transforms. Whether you're looking to unwind with a quiet drink by the lake or dance the night away in a vibrant club, Zell am See offers a variety of nightlife and entertainment options that cater to every taste. Having experienced the town's after-dark atmosphere firsthand, I'm excited to guide you through the best spots to explore when the day ends and the night begins.

14.1 Best Bars, Clubs, and Lounges

Zell am See's nightlife is an eclectic mix of laid-back lounges, cozy bars, and lively clubs. Whether you want to sip cocktails while overlooking the lake or dive into the heart of a buzzing dance floor, you'll find the perfect venue to match your mood.

Lakefront Lounges & Cocktail Bars

For a night out that combines stunning views with expertly crafted cocktails, Zell am See's lakeside bars are a must-visit. One of my personal favorites is Seevilla Freiberg, which sits right by the water and offers a serene atmosphere with breathtaking lake views.

The elegant yet relaxed vibe here makes it the perfect spot to start your evening.

- **What to try**: Their signature cocktails, particularly the Zeller Sour, which combines local ingredients with a twist on the classic Whiskey Sour.

- **Travel Tip**: If you're visiting in summer, try to arrive just before sunset to enjoy the golden hour and stunning reflections of the mountains on the lake.

Charming Pubs and Cozy Bars

For those who prefer a more intimate and traditional setting, Zell am See has a number of charming pubs and cozy bars perfect for unwinding after a long day of sightseeing. The Schneekristall Bar, located in the heart of the town, is a hidden gem that captures the rustic alpine charm. With its warm wooden interiors and friendly atmosphere, it's a great spot for enjoying a local beer or schnapps.

- **What to try**: Local beers, such as Zell am See Märzen, or a glass of Schnapps, a traditional Austrian spirit.

- **Travel Tip**: Don't be shy about engaging with the locals. Austrian pubs are known for their sociable atmospheres, and you may just make a new friend over a pint.

Clubbing in Zell am See

When the night calls for dancing, Club Stegen is the place to be. This vibrant club offers an energetic atmosphere, with both local and international DJs spinning dance tracks. The pulsating lights, infectious beats, and international crowd create an unforgettable experience.

- **What to try**: Grab a cocktail at the bar and head straight to the dance floor for a night of high-energy fun.
- **Travel Tip**: If you're planning to party at Club Stegen, be prepared to stay up late Austria's club scene often goes into the early morning hours.

14.2 Live Music & Theaters

If you're someone who enjoys live performances, Zell am See offers plenty of options that bring both classical music and modern performances to life. The town's cultural scene, though more intimate than major cities, still offers exceptional live music and theater that can transport you to another world.

Classical Music and Concerts

Zell am See is a town with a deep appreciation for classical music, and there are plenty of opportunities to enjoy it live.

One of the standout venues is The Kurhaus, a historic building nestled in the heart of the town. The Kurhaus regularly hosts classical concerts, from orchestral performances to intimate piano recitals, often in the picturesque setting of its grand hall.

- **What to try**: Check the schedule ahead of your visit for concerts that feature local talent or renowned classical artists.

- **Travel Tip**: The Kurhaus offers a great opportunity to experience the elegance of Austrian musical traditions in a historic venue, so be sure to dress up for the occasion.

Live Music Venues

For a more contemporary musical experience, head to The Grand Zell am See. This stylish venue offers a range of live music performances, from acoustic sets to jazz bands and everything in between. Located in the heart of the town, it's the perfect place to enjoy a relaxed evening with excellent music.

- **What to try**: The cocktails here are crafted with care, but be sure to try the local apple schnapps for a true taste of the region.

- **Travel Tip**: Check the event calendar as this venue often hosts live music sessions that feature both international and local talent.

Theater Performances

For those who appreciate a good play or performance, Zell am See also offers an impressive selection of theatrical events. The Kulturforum Zell am See is the go-to venue for everything from drama performances to dance shows. It's a cultural hub where both local and international artists come together to stage fascinating productions.

- **What to try**: See if you can catch a Bavarian or Austrian folk play, as they offer a unique glimpse into the region's history and traditions.

- **Travel Tip**: If you're not fluent in German, be sure to check if there are any performances with English subtitles or be ready for a charming experience in a foreign language.

14.3 Unique Nighttime Experiences

Zell am See is full of surprises after the sun sets. Beyond the bars, clubs, and music venues, there are several unique nighttime activities that offer a different kind of entertainment, allowing you to explore the town and its surroundings in a whole new light.

Night Skiing in Zell am See

For an unforgettable experience, try night skiing at the Schmittenhöhe ski resort, located just above Zell am See.

The resort offers night skiing on select runs, where the slopes are illuminated under the stars, creating an otherworldly, magical atmosphere. Gliding down the mountain with the city lights twinkling below is something every skier or snowboarder should experience at least once.

- **What to try**: Hit the slopes after dark and enjoy the peaceful yet exhilarating sensation of night skiing.

- **Travel Tip**: Night skiing is typically available from December to March, depending on snow conditions, so check ahead to plan your adventure.

Stargazing by the Lake

If you're looking for a more tranquil nighttime experience, consider a visit to the lakeside after dark. Zell am See offers some of the clearest skies, perfect for stargazing. The calm waters of Lake Zell provide a mirror-like reflection of the night sky, creating an unforgettable view. Bring a blanket and some hot cocoa, and let the stars guide your thoughts.

- **What to try**: Find a quiet spot along the lake and take in the natural beauty around you as the sky changes color at night.

- **Travel Tip**: Summer months offer the clearest skies, but the fall and winter months offer the added benefit of crisp air and fewer crowds, making it the perfect time for some peaceful solitude.

Lake Zell Night Cruise

One of the most unique ways to experience Zell am See at night is aboard a night cruise on the lake. Several local companies offer evening boat rides that allow you to take in the stunning scenery of the lake and surrounding mountains under the stars. These cruises are often paired with dinner or cocktails, making it a perfect romantic experience or a relaxing night out with friends.

- **What to try**: Treat yourself to a dinner cruise, where you can savor traditional Austrian cuisine as you cruise through the calm waters of Lake Zell.

- **Travel Tip**: Be sure to book in advance, as these cruises are popular, especially during peak seasons like summer and the holiday months.

Whether you're seeking a lively night of dancing, a sophisticated evening of classical music, or a serene moment by the lakeside, Zell am See has something for everyone when the sun goes down.

From vibrant bars and live performances to unique activities like night skiing and stargazing, there's no shortage of ways to make the most of your nights in this picturesque Austrian town. So, as you plan your trip, don't forget to carve out time for the nightlife; you won't regret it.

Chapter 15: Travel Tips & Safety Guide

Zell am See, with its stunning alpine landscapes and quaint charm, offers a serene escape for travelers. But like any destination, it's important to be prepared and informed so that your trip is not only enjoyable but also safe. In this chapter, I'll share essential travel tips to help you navigate this picturesque town smoothly, including key safety advice, cultural insights, and practical recommendations to ensure your visit is as effortless as it is memorable.

15.1 Local Laws & Travel Regulations

Before you pack your bags and head off to Zell am See, it's important to understand some local laws and regulations that might differ from those in your home country. While Austria is known for being friendly and welcoming, being aware of the rules will help you respect local customs and avoid any unintentional missteps.

Respect for Quiet Hours

Austria places a high value on quiet hours, especially in residential areas. Generally, quiet hours are enforced between 10 p.m.

and 6 a.m., meaning that loud noises, such as partying or construction work, should be avoided during this time. This is especially important if you're staying in a hotel or apartment building.

- **Travel Tip**: Be mindful of noise when walking through residential streets or enjoying a late-night snack in the town center. Your neighbors will certainly appreciate it.

Smoking Regulations

Smoking is banned in many indoor public spaces, including restaurants, bars, and cafes. However, designated smoking areas are typically provided, and outdoor terraces often allow smoking.

- **Travel Tip**: If you smoke, always look for the designated smoking areas before lighting up. Not only is it courteous, but it's also a legal requirement.

Speed Limits & Alcohol Laws

The legal driving speed limit is 50 km/h within towns, while highways usually have a limit of 130 km/h. As for alcohol, the legal drinking age is 16 for beer and wine, and 18 for spirits.

- **Travel Tip**: Always adhere to local traffic rules, and be extra cautious if you plan to rent a car in the area. In Austria, driving under the influence is taken very seriously, and fines can be hefty.

Littering Laws

Austria prides itself on being clean and environmentally conscious. Littering is strictly prohibited and could result in a fine.

- **Travel Tip**: Always dispose of your trash properly, and if you're unsure, look for recycling bins that are prevalent throughout the town.

15.2 Common Scams & Tourist Traps to Avoid

While Zell am See is generally a safe and welcoming place, like any popular tourist destination, it has its share of scams and tourist traps. Knowing how to spot these will help you stay ahead and avoid any unpleasant surprises during your trip.

Overpriced Souvenirs

Zell am See's charming shops offer a range of locally-made goods, but be cautious of overpriced souvenirs targeted at tourists. It's easy to get caught up in the excitement and pick up a trinket that's far more expensive than it should be.

- **Travel Tip**: For authentic and reasonably priced souvenirs, seek out local markets or smaller shops that are off the beaten path. They often offer better prices and unique, handmade items.

Tourist Taxis

Taxis in Zell am See can be convenient, but be aware of unmarked taxis or private drivers that may charge inflated fares. Always ensure the taxi is metered or agree on a fare before getting into the vehicle.

- **Travel Tip**: If you want to save money, consider using public transportation or ride-sharing apps like Bolt or Uber, where prices are fixed and transparent.

Street Performers and Beggars

Like many other tourist destinations, you'll encounter street performers and beggars in the more crowded areas of Zell am See. While most of these individuals are harmless, it's best to be cautious when approached by anyone asking for money.

- **Travel Tip**: If you're feeling generous, give directly to those in need through reputable organizations, rather than handing out cash to street performers.

Avoiding "Free" Tours

Some companies might offer "free" tours or "discounted" experiences that are later followed by hard sales tactics or hidden fees.

- **Travel Tip**: Always read reviews before booking any activities or tours. A great way to find trustworthy services is to use well-established platforms like TripAdvisor or GetYourGuide, where previous travelers share their experiences.

15.3 Emergency Contacts & Medical Facilities

While Zell am See is a safe place, it's always good to know what to do in case of an emergency. Here's a quick guide to help you stay prepared.

Emergency Numbers

Austria's emergency services are easily accessible with the following numbers:

- Police: 133
- Ambulance/Medical: 144
- Fire Department: 122
- Roadside Assistance: 120

- **Travel Tip**: In case of emergency, don't hesitate to call these numbers for immediate help. English is widely spoken by emergency responders in Austria.

Medical Facilities

If you require medical attention, Zell am See has several health clinics and pharmacies. The Zell am See Hospital offers emergency care, while local pharmacies are well-stocked with common over-the-counter medicines. The town's pharmacists often speak English and are very helpful when it comes to providing advice or medications.

- **Travel Tip**: Always travel with a basic first-aid kit that includes essentials like band-aids, pain relievers, and any prescribed medication you may need. Pharmacies in Austria are great, but it's always convenient to have your basics on hand.

Pharmacies & Prescriptions

Pharmacies in Zell am See are easily accessible, and most are open during business hours. However, if you need medication or prescriptions, note that you may need to show your prescription, especially for certain drugs.

- **Travel Tip**: If you're on regular medication, be sure to carry enough for the duration of your stay and get a translation of your prescription if needed.

15.4 Must-Have Apps & Local Services

To make your time in Zell am See as seamless as possible, here are a few essential apps and services you'll want to have at your fingertips.

Transport Apps

- **ÖBB (Austrian Federal Railways)**: This app is a must if you plan on traveling by train in Austria. It provides real-time updates on schedules and ticket booking.

- **Bus & Train Timetable**: This app helps you navigate the local bus and train systems around Zell am See and neighboring areas.

- **Travel Tip**: If you're planning on taking public transport often, the Zell am See Card gives you access to discounted or free rides on buses, boats, and cable cars, plus entrance to local attractions.

Language Apps

While many Austrians speak excellent English, downloading a translation app can still come in handy, especially when you're in smaller towns or trying to understand menu items or signs.

- **Google Translate**: An indispensable app when navigating language barriers, it works offline if you download the language packs in advance.

- **Duolingo**: If you want to try picking up some German phrases before your trip, Duolingo's fun, interactive lessons can be a great resource.

Cashless Payments

Austria is a cash-based society, but credit and debit cards are widely accepted in most places. However, it's always a good idea to carry some cash with you, particularly for smaller establishments like cafes or local markets.

- **Travel Tip**: Apps like Apple Pay or Google Pay are commonly accepted in shops and restaurants, making it easier for you to pay on the go without needing to handle cash.

Weather Apps

The weather in Zell am See can change rapidly, so having a reliable weather app will help you plan your outdoor adventures and stay safe in case of sudden weather changes.

- **Weather Pro**: This app provides detailed, up-to-the-minute forecasts for Zell am See, so you can stay prepared for rain, snow, or sunshine.

By staying informed about local laws, avoiding common scams, knowing emergency contacts, and using the right apps, you can ensure that your trip to Zell am See is as smooth and safe as possible. The town is welcoming, well-equipped, and easy to navigate, making it the perfect destination for both first-time and seasoned travelers. With these tips in hand, you can focus on enjoying everything Zell am See has to offer from its charming streets to its stunning natural landscapes. Safe travels!

Chapter 16: Budgeting & Money Matters

When I first visited Zell am See, I was captivated by its charming atmosphere, but I soon realized that while the town is a serene retreat, its appeal also comes with its own set of financial considerations. From cozy alpine chalets to lakeside cafes, Zell am See offers a range of experiences suited for different budgets. However, knowing how to navigate the money matters whether you're a backpacker on a shoestring budget or someone looking for luxury, can make your trip all the more enjoyable. In this chapter, I'll share everything you need to know about budgeting for your stay in Zell am See.

16.1 Currency Exchange & Payment Options

Zell am See, like the rest of Austria, uses the Euro (EUR) as its currency. Whether you're arriving from the US, the UK, or any other part of the world, it's important to understand how to manage your finances while traveling in Austria.

Currency Exchange

If you're arriving from outside the Eurozone, the most straightforward way to exchange your currency for Euros is through international airports or local currency exchange offices. Zell am See itself has a few currency exchange services, but you'll generally get better rates in larger cities like Salzburg or Vienna.

- **Travel Tip**: Avoid exchanging money at airports unless absolutely necessary, as the rates are usually less favorable. If you can, withdraw cash from ATMs in Zell am See for a more competitive exchange rate.

Credit & Debit Cards

Credit and debit cards are widely accepted in Zell am See. Most hotels, restaurants, and shops will take cards, including Visa, Mastercard, and American Express. However, it's still a good idea to carry a bit of cash, especially for smaller shops, markets, or rural establishments.

- **Travel Tip**: Be sure to inform your bank about your travel plans before you leave so they don't block your card due to foreign transactions. Also, check if your bank charges foreign transaction fees, which can add up.

ATMs

ATMs are abundant in Zell am See, and most will allow you to withdraw cash directly from your bank account in Euros. Just be mindful of ATM fees, which can range from €2 to €5 per withdrawal, depending on your bank.

- **Travel Tip**: Use debit cards that offer free international ATM withdrawals, or consider getting a prepaid travel card, which often offers better exchange rates and fewer fees.

Mobile Payments

Mobile payment systems like Apple Pay and Google Pay are gaining traction in Zell am See. Many cafes, shops, and restaurants accept these payment options, making it convenient to pay without carrying physical cards or cash.

- **Travel Tip**: Ensure your phone is set up to use mobile payments before arriving. This can save time and hassle, especially for small transactions or when you're in a hurry.

16.2 Cost of Living & Budget Breakdown

Zell am See is not the cheapest destination in Austria, but with a little planning, you can experience everything the town has to offer without breaking the bank.

The cost of living here is generally lower than in major cities like Vienna, but it can still vary depending on the time of year and your lifestyle.

Accommodation

Zell am See offers a range of accommodation options, from budget hostels to luxurious lakeside resorts. Here's a breakdown of the costs:

- **Budget Accommodation**: Hostels and guesthouses typically range from €30 to €60 per night for a dorm bed or simple private room. If you book in advance, you can sometimes find deals or packages.

- **Mid-Range Accommodation**: Hotels and boutique guesthouses in the €80 to €150 per night range offer more comfort and amenities like breakfast and Wi-Fi.

- **Luxury Accommodation**: For a more indulgent stay, you can expect to pay €200+ per night at high-end hotels or lakeside resorts with full-service spas, restaurants, and prime locations.

- **Travel Tip**: Book early, especially during peak tourist seasons (summer and winter), when demand is higher and prices can soar.

Food & Drink

Zell am See's food scene offers everything from hearty alpine meals to elegant fine dining. The cost of meals can vary depending on whether you're dining at a casual cafe or a Michelin-starred restaurant.

- **Budget Meals**: You can find affordable meals at local cafes or street food stalls for around €8 to €15 for a simple dish like a schnitzel or a local sausage. A quick lunch at a bakery or small restaurant might cost €5 to €10.

- **Mid-Range Dining**: A three-course meal at a mid-range restaurant could cost you between €20 to €40 per person. The town has several restaurants offering authentic Austrian fare with a twist, and you'll find good wine pairings at an extra €5 to €10 per glass.

- **Fine Dining**: If you're looking to indulge, a high-end dinner at a lakeside restaurant could easily set you back €50 to €100+ per person, especially if you order wine pairings or specialty dishes.

- **Travel Tip**: To save on meals, consider shopping at the local supermarkets like Billa or Spar, where you can purchase fresh ingredients and prepare your own meals.

It's a great way to keep costs low while enjoying a more local experience.

Transportation

Zell am See is small enough to walk around, but if you want to explore the surrounding areas, public transportation is readily available. The Zell am See Card offers discounted or free access to buses, boats, and cable cars.

- **Bus and Train**: A bus ride within Zell am See costs around €2 to €3 one-way. Trains to nearby towns like Kaprun or Salzburg typically cost €5 to €20, depending on the distance.

- **Car Rental**: If you prefer to rent a car, expect to pay €40 to €70 per day, depending on the car type and rental company. Gas prices in Austria are comparable to the rest of Europe.

- **Travel Tip**: If you plan on using the local buses, consider getting a Zell am See Card for discounts on public transport, activities, and entrance fees to attractions like the Kitzsteinhorn Glacier.

Attractions

- Outdoor activities, such as hiking, are often free or low-cost, especially if you have a Zell am See Card. For example, cable cars might cost around €20 to €30 per person, but with the card, you can enjoy significant discounts.

- Cultural sites, such as museums and galleries, charge entrance fees that range from €5 to €15.

- **Travel Tip**: Always check if there's a discounted pass or combined ticket for multiple attractions. The Zell am See Card often offers good value for money if you plan on visiting several activities.

16.3 Saving Money & Travel Hacks

No matter what your budget is, there are always clever ways to save money during your trip to Zell am See.

Book in Advance

One of the best ways to save money is to book your accommodation, tours, and transportation in advance. During peak seasons, prices can increase significantly, so securing everything ahead of time can help you avoid last-minute price hikes.

- **Travel Tip**: Use booking sites that allow you to compare prices, such as Booking.com, Airbnb, or Expedia. Be sure to read reviews before confirming your booking.

Take Advantage of Free Activities

Zell am See is known for its stunning natural beauty, and much of what makes it special like hiking, swimming, or strolling through its picturesque streets is completely free. The surrounding nature is perfect for a relaxing day outdoors without spending a dime.

- **Travel Tip**: Ask locals for hidden gems whether it's a quiet spot on the lake for a swim or a secluded hiking trail with panoramic views.

Eat Like a Local

Avoid overpriced tourist traps by heading to where the locals eat. Ask your hotel concierge or hosts for restaurant recommendations away from the busy tourist areas. Street food, bakeries, and local markets are often great options for an affordable, authentic meal.

- **Travel Tip**: If you're staying in an apartment or Airbnb, cooking some of your own meals can save you a lot of money, especially for breakfasts and picnics.

Use Discount Passes

The Zell am See Card is essential for anyone staying in the region for more than a couple of days. It offers free or discounted access to public transportation, cable cars, and local attractions. The savings quickly add up, especially if you plan to do a lot of sightseeing.

- **Travel Tip**: If you're traveling during the off-season, check for special deals on the Zell am See Card or other regional passes that can provide even more value.

Zell am See offers a variety of experiences for travelers with all kinds of budgets. Whether you're looking for affordable meals, budget-friendly accommodation, or a luxury experience, this charming alpine town has something for everyone. By planning ahead, taking advantage of local discounts, and being mindful of your spending, you can enjoy all the beauty Zell am See has to offer without overspending. Whether you're strolling along the lake, hiking in the mountains, or enjoying the local cuisine, your time here will be filled with unforgettable memories without breaking the bank.

Chapter 17: Luxury Travel & Exclusive Experiences

Zell am See is a town of sublime contrasts, where the rugged beauty of the Alps meets the sophisticated charm of lakeside luxury. While the town welcomes all kinds of travelers, for those seeking an exceptional, high-end escape, Zell am See provides an array of experiences that are nothing short of extraordinary.

In this chapter, we will dive into the realm of luxury travel, showcasing exclusive hotels, private tours, and indulgent dining that will make your stay unforgettable. Whether you're celebrating a special occasion or simply treating yourself to the finer things in life, this chapter will guide you through the best that Zell am See has to offer for the discerning traveler.

17.1 High-End Hotels & Resorts

For those who want to combine alpine adventure with world-class comfort, Zell am See has a selection of luxurious accommodations that provide the perfect base for your indulgent getaway. From lakeside resorts offering sweeping views to mountainside chalets designed with the utmost attention to detail, these properties offer an experience far beyond the ordinary.

Schlosshotel Fuschl

Set in a 15th-century castle on the shores of Lake Fuschl, Schlosshotel Fuschl is one of the most luxurious hotels in the Zell am See region. This fairy-tale castle has been transformed into a five-star resort, blending historical grandeur with modern elegance. The rooms and suites are spacious, offering breathtaking views of the surrounding lake and mountains. The hotel's private spa, featuring an indoor pool, sauna, and wellness treatments, ensures that guests are pampered in style.

- **Travel Tip**: Book a lake-view room for the most stunning sunrise and sunset experiences. It's worth the splurge for the view alone!

Grand Hotel Zell am See

Located on the banks of Lake Zell, Grand Hotel Zell am See is the epitome of lakeside luxury. With its historical architecture and modern amenities, this five-star hotel has been a symbol of elegance since the 19th century.

Rooms feature classic decor, and many come with large windows that offer mesmerizing views of the lake or the surrounding mountains. Guests can enjoy exquisite fine dining at the hotel's restaurants or unwind at the full-service spa with a panoramic view.

- **Travel Tip**: Don't miss the Hotel's private boat for a peaceful cruise on Lake Zell. It's a perfect way to appreciate the stunning scenery in private, away from the crowds.

InterContinental Resort Zell am See

If you're seeking a true luxury experience with a global brand's touch, the InterContinental Resort Zell am See offers nothing less than excellence. This five-star resort combines the grandeur of the Austrian Alps with the sleek sophistication of a global hotel chain. The resort features an expansive spa, an indoor-outdoor swimming pool, and a variety of dining options that focus on fine, seasonal Austrian cuisine.

- **Travel Tip**: If you're looking to indulge in some après-ski activities, the InterContinental has a private ski shuttle that will take you directly to the slopes. There's no better way to start your winter adventure.

17.2 Private Tours & VIP Access

For those who seek a deeper, more personalized connection to the area, Zell am See offers a range of exclusive tours and VIP experiences that allow you to see the region from a whole new perspective. From private sightseeing tours to helicopter rides, these bespoke services ensure that you get the most out of your luxury trip.

Private Guided Tours

If you're interested in immersing yourself in the culture and history of Zell am See without the crowds, a private guided tour is the perfect choice. Several companies offer tailor-made experiences, ranging from cultural tours of Zell am See's medieval town center to full-day excursions exploring the nearby villages of Kaprun or Kitzsteinhorn Glacier. Your guide will cater the tour to your specific interests, whether you want to learn about the region's history, experience the local traditions, or explore hidden gems off the beaten path.

- **Travel Tip**: Consider hiring a private guide who can tailor the experience to your personal preferences. For history lovers, a tour focused on the medieval castles around the region can provide fascinating insights.

Private Boat Tours on Lake Zell

One of the most magical ways to experience Zell am See's natural beauty is by boat. Chartering a private boat on Lake Zell offers a serene and exclusive way to enjoy the stunning scenery. Whether you're looking for a romantic sunset cruise or a half-day excursion around the lake, many operators offer personalized boat tours with onboard service. You can even arrange for a private chef to prepare a gourmet meal during your journey, enhancing your lakeside experience.

- **Travel Tip**: For the ultimate VIP experience, ask for a sailing yacht with a skipper. Enjoy the peace of the water and the luxury of total privacy as you glide past the majestic mountains.

Helicopter Tours

For the ultimate in exclusivity and grandeur, nothing compares to a helicopter tour over the Alps. These tours give you an unparalleled bird's-eye view of Zell am See, the surrounding lakes, and the snow-capped peaks of the Kitzsteinhorn Glacier. A helicopter tour is an adrenaline-pumping way to take in the stunning landscape, and you can even arrange for a stop at a mountain hut for a gourmet lunch in the sky.

- **Travel Tip**: Helicopter tours can be quite expensive, so if you're looking to save on costs, consider sharing the experience with a small group to split the price while still maintaining a private feel.

17.3 Michelin-Star Restaurants & Fine Dining

Zell am See is home to some truly exceptional restaurants where culinary artistry meets the finest ingredients. If you're a foodie who appreciates the finer things in life, you'll find plenty of world-class dining options to indulge your palate.

Restaurant Kupferkessel

For an unforgettable fine dining experience in Zell am See, Restaurant Kupferkessel is a must-visit. This Michelin-starred gem specializes in traditional Austrian cuisine with a contemporary twist. The intimate ambiance, attentive service, and exquisite wine list make it the perfect setting for a special evening. The tasting menu changes seasonally, ensuring that each visit brings something new to savor.

- **Travel Tip**: Be sure to try the Kaiserschmarrn, a traditional Austrian dessert. It's a sweet, fluffy pancake dish that's both rich and indulgent, the perfect way to end your meal.

Das Voglhaus

Another exceptional fine dining destination in Zell am See is Das Voglhaus, a charming yet upscale restaurant that serves modern interpretations of classic Austrian dishes. The chef sources ingredients locally, ensuring that the food is always fresh and of the highest quality. With an extensive wine list and a cozy, refined atmosphere, Das Voglhaus is an ideal spot for a gourmet dinner.

- **Travel Tip**: Pair your meal with a bottle of Austrian wine. The country's vineyards, particularly in the Wachau Valley, produce world-class wines that will elevate any dish.

Hotel St. Georg Restaurant

The Hotel St. Georg Restaurant offers a truly exceptional fine dining experience. Nestled in the heart of Zell am See, this restaurant boasts a Michelin-starred menu that combines the best of Austrian ingredients with a global culinary flair. From the moment you step inside, you're transported into a world of sophistication and flavor. Every dish is thoughtfully prepared and elegantly presented, making it a feast for both the eyes and the taste buds.

- **Travel Tip**: Make a reservation in advance, especially during the busy winter and summer seasons. A window seat will allow you to enjoy not only the gourmet food but also the magnificent lake views.

Zell am See offers an array of luxurious experiences that will make any discerning traveler feel truly special. From staying at world-class resorts and enjoying private boat rides to indulging in Michelin-star dining, the town provides exclusive moments that elevate your vacation to the extraordinary. Whether you're celebrating an anniversary, escaping for a romantic getaway, or simply seeking to indulge in the finer things in life, Zell am See's combination of natural beauty and opulent experiences makes it a truly unparalleled destination.

The next time you're planning a luxurious escape, let this town's charm and elegance sweep you off your feet you won't be disappointed.

Chapter 18: Solo Traveler's Guide

Traveling solo is a liberating, transformative experience that allows you to connect deeply with the destination, its people, and your own sense of adventure. Zell am See, with its combination of natural beauty, historical charm, and friendly atmosphere, is the perfect place for solo travelers seeking a balance of exploration, relaxation, and discovery. Whether you're traveling to unwind, seek adventure, or explore local culture at your own pace, Zell am See offers plenty of opportunities to do so. In this chapter, I'll provide valuable tips, insights, and recommendations to make your solo trip both enjoyable and safe.

18.1 Safety Tips & Precautions

One of the greatest concerns for solo travelers is safety, but Zell am See is known for being a peaceful and welcoming town. While it's certainly a very safe destination, there are still a few precautions you can take to ensure your trip goes smoothly.

General Safety Advice

- **Stay Aware of Your Surroundings**: Zell am See is a safe place, but like any tourist destination, it's important to stay alert, especially when you're in more crowded areas.

Pay attention to your belongings and avoid leaving valuables in plain sight.

- **Trust Your Instincts**: If something feels off, it's always a good idea to remove yourself from the situation. Whether you're exploring the town or taking a hike in the mountains, your gut instinct is a reliable guide.

- **Emergency Numbers**: The local emergency number in Austria is 112, which will connect you to police, medical, or fire services. It's also good to know the location of the nearest hospital in case of any unforeseen accidents.

- **Secure Your Accommodation**: Always lock doors and windows when you're inside your hotel room or accommodation. Many accommodations also offer in-room safes, so make use of them for storing your passport and other valuables.

- **Night Travel**: Zell am See is generally safe at night, but as a solo traveler, it's wise to stick to well-lit streets and avoid walking alone in isolated areas after dark. Use taxis or local rideshare services if you're heading out late.

Health Precautions

- **Stay Hydrated & Eat Well**: Zell am See is a place for outdoor activities, and you'll be walking, hiking, and possibly skiing, so it's essential to stay hydrated and fuel your body with nutritious meals. Don't forget to carry water with you when heading out for a day of exploration.

- **Travel Insurance**: While not unique to Zell am See, having comprehensive travel insurance is always a good idea, especially if you're engaging in outdoor activities. Make sure it covers medical emergencies, including evacuation if necessary.

- **Know the Local Pharmacies**: Pharmacies in Austria are well-stocked, and many pharmacists speak English. It's useful to know where the nearest pharmacy is in case you need any basic health supplies during your stay.

18.2 Best Places for Solo Travelers

Zell am See offers a mix of tranquil spots for reflection, as well as plenty of social spaces where you can meet fellow travelers. Whether you seek peaceful lakeside strolls or more active pursuits, there's something for every solo adventurer here.

Lake Zell

There's no better way to spend your solo time in Zell am See than walking along the picturesque shores of Lake Zell. The lake's crystal-clear waters reflect the towering mountains, creating a sense of calm that will wash over you. Whether you're taking a quiet early-morning stroll or sitting on one of the benches along the promenade, Lake Zell provides a peaceful setting for contemplation or people-watching. Don't forget to bring your camera there's beauty at every turn.

- **Must-Do**: Hire a small boat for a solo adventure on the lake. The solitude of the water, combined with the magnificent views of the mountains, creates a feeling of complete tranquility.

Schmittenhöhe Mountain

For those seeking a bit more adventure, Schmittenhöhe Mountain is the perfect destination. Take a cable car ride up the mountain for panoramic views of Zell am See, the lake, and the surrounding Alpine peaks. Solo hikers can explore the various trails, which cater to different skill levels. Whether you're trekking through the lush forests or hiking up to one of the summit viewpoints, Schmittenhöhe offers plenty of opportunities to lose yourself in nature.

- **Travel Tip**: If you're an avid hiker, try the Gipfel Trail for a more challenging route. The views from the top are nothing short of breathtaking, and the sense of accomplishment you'll feel after reaching the summit is something you won't forget.

Zell am See Old Town

For solo travelers who enjoy immersing themselves in culture, Zell am See's Old Town is a charming, walkable area to explore at your own pace. The cobbled streets, quaint shops, and historic buildings provide a glimpse into the town's rich past. While it's perfect for wandering and getting lost in, make sure to stop at the St. Hippolyte's Church and the Zell am See Castle, both of which offer a peaceful escape and fascinating local history.

- **Must-Do**: Treat yourself to a leisurely coffee at one of the cafes in the main square. Take the time to people-watch or chat with friendly locals who are often happy to share stories about the area.

Kitzsteinhorn Glacier

If you're visiting in the winter or love snow-covered landscapes, take a trip to Kitzsteinhorn Glacier. The glacier offers year-round skiing, but it's also a great place to simply enjoy the stunning Alpine environment.

Solo travelers can take a cable car to the top and walk around the Top of Salzburg platform, which provides panoramic views of the surrounding mountains. It's a breathtaking experience and one that will provide plenty of opportunity for solitude.

- **Travel Tip**: For solo skiers, consider booking a ski instructor for a day to make the most of your time on the slopes.

18.3 How to Meet Fellow Travelers & Locals

One of the joys of solo travel is the opportunity to meet new people, whether they are fellow travelers or friendly locals. Zell am See offers plenty of chances for socializing, from lively bars to communal hiking groups.

Cafes and Restaurants

While Zell am See may not have a nightlife scene as bustling as bigger cities, the town is full of charming cafes and eateries where you can strike up a conversation. Many cafes have communal tables, perfect for meeting fellow travelers. If you're a foodie, try some of the traditional Austrian dishes, and don't be afraid to ask for recommendations from locals they are often eager to share insights about the area.

- **Must-Do**: Visit Konditorei-Café Zisser, a popular spot among locals, for a slice of cake and a coffee.

It's cozy and often filled with both residents and tourists, making it a great place for conversation.

Join a Group Tour

One of the easiest ways to meet people while traveling solo is by joining a group activity. Whether it's a hiking tour, a cooking class, or a guided boat ride, Zell am See offers plenty of group experiences where you can meet fellow adventurers. Not only does it enhance your experience, but it also gives you a chance to share the journey with others.

- **Travel Tip**: Consider taking a photography tour of the town or surrounding landscape. It's a fantastic way to bond with others while enjoying Zell am See's stunning vistas.

Attend Local Events

Keep an eye on the local event calendar during your stay, as Zell am See hosts various festivals, live music, and cultural events throughout the year. From traditional Austrian folk music performances to food and wine festivals, these events are perfect for solo travelers who want to meet new people and enjoy the lively atmosphere of the town.

- **Must-Do**: Check out the Zeller See Festival if you're visiting during the summer. It's a lively event that attracts both locals and tourists, and it offers an excellent opportunity to socialize.

Zell am See is a dream destination for solo travelers, offering a blend of adventure, relaxation, and cultural exploration. Whether you're hiking the majestic mountains, reflecting by the tranquil lake, or immersing yourself in the local culture, you'll find plenty of opportunities to connect with yourself and others. By taking the right safety precautions, exploring the best solo spots, and embracing local experiences, your time in Zell am See will undoubtedly be a fulfilling, unforgettable adventure. Enjoy every moment after all, solo travel is about finding freedom, and Zell am See is the perfect place to do just that.

Chapter 19: Family & Kid-Friendly Travel

Traveling with children can be an immensely rewarding experience, but it also requires a bit more thought and preparation. Luckily, Zell am See offers a wide array of family-friendly activities, attractions, and accommodations, ensuring that both kids and adults alike have an unforgettable time. With its picturesque landscapes, outdoor adventures, and cultural gems, this charming Austrian town is perfect for family getaways. In this chapter, I'll guide you through the best spots for kids, provide insights into where to stay and eat, and offer practical tips to help make your trip smooth and enjoyable for everyone.

19.1 Best Attractions for Kids

Zell am See is a destination where kids can enjoy both thrilling activities and quiet moments in nature. From exploring the great outdoors to learning about the local culture, the town has something to offer every member of the family.

Lake Zell & Water Sports

The sparkling waters of Lake Zell are one of the main draws for families, offering a variety of activities that kids can enjoy.

During the summer, the lake is perfect for swimming, boating, or simply enjoying a lakeside picnic. You can rent pedal boats or small motorboats, which is always a fun and easy way for families to spend time together on the water.

- **Tip for Families**: If your kids love water activities but you prefer to stay dry, consider taking a Lake Zell cruise. These gentle boat rides around the lake offer stunning views of the town and the surrounding mountains, and the kids will love being on the water without getting too wet.

Schmittenhöhe Mountain

For families that enjoy a good hike or simply want to explore the mountains, Schmittenhöhe is a must-visit. This mountain, accessible by cable car, offers breathtaking views of the region, and there are family-friendly walking trails suitable for all ages. The Schmittenhöhe family adventure trail is a highlight, designed specifically for kids, with interactive learning stations that teach them about the local flora, fauna, and history. It's a perfect mix of fun and education.

- **Tip for Families**: In the winter months, Schmittenhöhe turns into a winter wonderland, perfect for skiing or snowboarding. Kids can take beginner lessons at the ski school while parents enjoy the slopes.

Even if you're not into skiing, the snow-covered peaks provide a magical setting for family photos.

Zell am See Animal Park

If your children enjoy meeting animals, a visit to the Zell am See Animal Park is a must. Located just outside the town, the park is home to a variety of animals including deer, goats, and other Alpine wildlife. Kids can get up close and personal with the animals, and there's plenty of room for them to run and play. It's a great place to spend a few hours in nature, letting the kids explore while you relax.

- **Travel Tip**: Pack some snacks for a picnic in the park. There are several designated areas where you can sit down and enjoy a meal surrounded by nature.

Tauern Spa Kaprun

For a bit of relaxation and fun combined, Tauern Spa Kaprun is an excellent choice. This family-friendly spa offers a variety of pools, including some outdoor ones with incredible views of the mountains. It's the perfect place to unwind after a busy day of sightseeing. The spa is designed with families in mind, and there are areas specifically for children to play and swim, making it a wonderful spot for parents to relax while the kids splash around.

- **Must-Do**: Don't miss the family spa area with its warm, shallow pools for kids and large water slides that will surely keep the little ones entertained for hours.

Kitzsteinhorn Glacier

If your family is visiting Zell am See in winter, the Kitzsteinhorn Glacier is a thrilling destination for kids. Aside from skiing, the glacier offers a range of family-friendly experiences. The Ice Arena and Top of Salzburg viewing platform are highlights, with spectacular views of the snowy Alps. Kids will love the chance to play in the snow and engage in snow-based activities, while adults can enjoy the stunning winter landscape.

- **Tip for Families**: The Kitzsteinhorn Snow Park offers a fun, interactive area for kids to enjoy snow tubing, building snowmen, and even taking part in fun, supervised activities.

19.2 Family-Friendly Accommodations & Restaurants

Finding accommodations that cater to the needs of families is key to a stress-free trip. Luckily, Zell am See offers a variety of family-friendly hotels, resorts, and restaurants that cater to children and parents alike.

Best Family Hotels

- **Grand Hotel Zell am See**: This lakeside hotel is perfect for families, offering spacious rooms and family suites with spectacular lake views. The hotel has a children's playroom, an outdoor playground, and easy access to the lake for water activities. It's also well-located, making it easy to explore the town on foot.

- **Hotel Salzburgerhof**: Another great family-friendly option, Hotel Salzburgerhof combines luxury and comfort with kid-friendly amenities like a kids' club, indoor and outdoor pools, and a large spa. The hotel even offers baby-sitting services, so parents can enjoy a little time to themselves while the kids are entertained.

- **Alpenpalace Luxury Hideaway & Spa**: For families looking for a more secluded and luxurious stay, the Alpenpalace offers a mix of spacious family rooms, a dedicated children's program, and an exclusive atmosphere. It's located close to both skiing areas and hiking trails, so there's something for everyone in the family.

Family-Friendly Restaurants

- **Pizzeria die Salzgrotte**: For a casual meal that the kids will love, this cozy pizzeria offers delicious pizzas and pasta, along with a friendly atmosphere that's perfect for families. The staff is welcoming to children, and there are plenty of options for picky eaters.

- **Restaurant Kupferkessel**: This charming, family-friendly restaurant serves hearty Austrian dishes in a relaxed setting. It's an excellent spot to try some traditional Austrian fare, with options like schnitzels, sausages, and strudels that even the pickiest of eaters will enjoy.

- **Seehotel Freiberg**: Located right by Lake Zell, this lakeside restaurant is great for families looking to enjoy a meal with a view. The outdoor seating area is perfect in the warmer months, and there's a kids' menu that caters to young tastes while offering the whole family a chance to enjoy fresh local ingredients.

19.3 Tips for Traveling with Children

Traveling with children, especially to a new place, can be both exciting and challenging. Here are some tips to make your experience in Zell am See as smooth and enjoyable as possible:

Pack Smart

When traveling with children, it's essential to pack strategically. Beyond the usual clothes and toiletries, make sure to bring items that will keep your kids entertained during long car rides, meals, or downtime. Consider bringing:

- Small toys, books, or travel games for entertainment.
- A compact stroller or carrier for younger children, especially if you're going to be hiking or exploring the town.
- Child-friendly snacks and drinks for when hunger strikes.

Stay Flexible

While it's important to have a plan for your trip, it's equally important to stay flexible. Children can be unpredictable, and sometimes they need downtime or a change of pace. Be prepared to adapt your itinerary if necessary, whether it's shortening a hike or adding in an extra stop for a fun activity.

Involve the Kids in Planning

When traveling as a family, it's helpful to let your children have a say in the trip. Ask them what activities or attractions interest them the most and try to incorporate their preferences into your itinerary. This way, they'll be more engaged and excited about the trip.

Take Breaks & Rest

Exploring Zell am See can be tiring, especially for little legs. Be sure to take breaks throughout the day. Resting in a park or enjoying a leisurely coffee break in a café can help both you and your kids recharge for the next adventure.

Zell am See is a fantastic family destination, offering a blend of outdoor activities, cultural exploration, and relaxation. Whether you're cruising on the lake, hiking up a mountain, or enjoying a cozy meal by the fire, this town is sure to provide lasting memories for families of all shapes and sizes. By choosing the right activities, accommodations, and dining options, you'll ensure a stress-free and enjoyable trip for both parents and children alike. With a little planning, Zell am See will quickly become a family favorite, one you'll return to again and again.

Chapter 20: Sustainable & Responsible Tourism

Traveling is a beautiful way to experience the world, but it's also important to remember that the places we visit are precious and need our care and respect. As we journey through the landscapes, cultures, and communities that make a destination unique, we must also consider how our travel choices impact the environment, local economies, and societies.

Zell am See, with its pristine natural beauty and rich cultural heritage, is a perfect destination to explore sustainably. In this chapter, I'll guide you through how you can enjoy this stunning Austrian gem while minimizing your environmental footprint and supporting local communities.

20.1 Eco-Friendly Accommodations & Tours

Zell am See is home to a growing number of eco-conscious accommodations and tours that allow you to enjoy the area responsibly. Whether you're staying in a charming mountain lodge or booking a sustainable tour, there are plenty of ways to support the local environment and reduce your impact on nature.

Eco-Friendly Hotels & Resorts

- **Schlosshotel Fuschl**: This luxurious hotel, located on the banks of Lake Fuschl, is committed to sustainable practices. They focus on reducing energy consumption, using environmentally friendly products, and promoting local food in their restaurant. The hotel offers the perfect blend of luxury and sustainability, making it an ideal choice for travelers who want to experience the beauty of Zell am See while maintaining eco-friendly standards.

- **Hotel Tirolerhof**: Nestled in the heart of Zell am See, Hotel Tirolerhof is another excellent option for eco-conscious travelers. This hotel places a strong emphasis on sustainability, using solar energy, recycling programs, and energy-efficient heating systems. They also work closely with local farmers to provide organic, locally sourced food that highlights the best of the region's produce.

- **Biohotel Stanglwirt**: While not located directly in Zell am See, Biohotel Stanglwirt in nearby Going is a shining example of eco-friendly hospitality. This five-star hotel has implemented a comprehensive sustainability strategy, including solar-powered heating, organic farming, and green building practices. Staying here is not only an indulgence but a commitment to sustainable luxury.

Eco-Tours & Activities

- **Electric Boat Tours on Lake Zell**: Instead of using gas-powered boats, why not take a scenic tour of Lake Zell aboard an electric boat? These eco-friendly tours reduce pollution and offer a peaceful, quiet way to experience the beauty of the lake and the surrounding mountains. Glide along the water with stunning views, all while reducing your carbon footprint.

- **Sustainable Hiking Tours**: Hiking in Zell am See is one of the best ways to experience the area's breathtaking landscapes, and there are several companies that offer guided eco-tours. These tours focus on sustainable hiking, emphasizing the preservation of local flora and fauna. Guides often provide insight into the environmental challenges the region faces and teach you about the importance of conservation.

- **Biking and Electric Biking**: For those who prefer cycling, Zell am See offers a variety of biking paths that are suitable for all levels. There are eco-friendly bike rentals available, including electric bikes for those who want a little extra assistance while exploring the area. This is a great way to reduce your carbon footprint while enjoying the town's stunning natural beauty.

20.2 Supporting Local Communities & Ethical Tourism

Responsible tourism isn't just about protecting the environment it's also about supporting the people who call the destination home. By engaging with local communities in a meaningful and respectful way, you can ensure that your visit has a positive impact on both the economy and the cultural heritage of Zell am See.

Shop Local

Zell am See is home to many small, family-owned businesses that offer handmade goods, local crafts, and regional produce. Shopping in local markets and stores not only helps support the local economy but also gives you the chance to bring home unique souvenirs that reflect the culture of the area. Whether it's handcrafted wooden items, local cheese, or alpine wool clothing, buying directly from local artisans ensures that your money goes directly into the hands of the people who create these beautiful products.

- **Must-Visit**: The Zell am See Market on Wednesdays is a fantastic opportunity to purchase fresh, local produce, as well as traditional goods. Vendors often offer organic vegetables, homemade honey, and other regional specialties. It's the perfect place to experience the town's culture and support local farmers.

Support Local Restaurants

Dining at locally-owned restaurants is another way to support the community while enjoying the authentic flavors of Zell am See. Many restaurants in the area use locally sourced ingredients, and by dining at these establishments, you're helping promote sustainable farming practices.

- **Where to Eat**: Consider dining at Restaurant Kupferkessel, where the chef focuses on fresh, local ingredients. Or try Seehotel Freiberg, which serves dishes made with seasonal produce from nearby farms. Supporting these restaurants ensures that you are part of a sustainable cycle that benefits both the environment and the local community.

Cultural Respect

Zell am See's culture is steeped in centuries of history, and one of the best ways to engage ethically with the local community is to respect local traditions and customs. Whether it's understanding Austrian table manners or participating in local festivals, showing appreciation for the culture will enrich your experience and foster positive connections with residents.

- **Cultural Tip**: If you're visiting during a local festival or event, take the time to learn about the tradition and participate with respect.

The Zeller See Fest is a fantastic cultural celebration, and by attending, you'll not only enjoy the festivities but also learn about the region's rich heritage.

20.3 Reducing Your Environmental Impact

In addition to supporting local businesses, there are many small steps you can take to reduce your overall environmental impact while visiting Zell am See. From transportation choices to waste reduction, every decision counts.

Sustainable Transportation

- **Public Transportation**: Zell am See has an excellent public transportation system that makes it easy to get around without relying on cars. Using trains, buses, or the town's efficient shuttle services helps reduce the carbon footprint associated with travel. Consider purchasing a Zell am See-Kaprun Card, which provides unlimited access to buses and trains in the region, along with discounts for local attractions.

- **Walking & Cycling**: Zell am See is a wonderfully walkable town, and many of the top attractions are within easy walking distance from one another. In addition, cycling is a great option for exploring the region in an eco-friendly way.

The town's bike-friendly infrastructure makes it simple to rent a bike and get around without contributing to pollution.

Waste Reduction

- **Carry Reusable Items**: A simple way to minimize waste while traveling is to use reusable items whenever possible. Bring a reusable water bottle to refill at the town's public fountains, which provide fresh and clean drinking water. Use reusable bags for shopping and try to avoid single-use plastics.

- **Eco-Friendly Packaging**: When shopping for souvenirs or eating at local restaurants, be mindful of packaging. Many shops in Zell am See offer eco-friendly alternatives, and some restaurants are reducing waste by using compostable packaging or offering discounts for bringing your own containers.

Conservation Efforts

Zell am See is nestled in a natural paradise, and the town works hard to preserve its natural surroundings. As a traveler, you can contribute by following Leave No Trace principles: stick to marked trails, avoid disturbing wildlife, and take your trash with you when exploring the wilderness.

If you're participating in outdoor activities, consider working with tour operators that emphasize environmental education and responsible behavior.

- **Travel Tip**: If you're hiking or exploring the mountains, consider booking a Guided Nature Tour. These tours often highlight the importance of preserving local ecosystems and teach you about sustainable practices.

Sustainable tourism isn't just a buzzword it's a way of traveling that enriches both the destination and the traveler. Zell am See offers plenty of opportunities to enjoy the region responsibly, from staying at eco-friendly hotels to supporting local businesses and reducing your environmental footprint.

As a visitor, your choices can make a big difference, not just for the environment but for the people who call Zell am See home. By choosing sustainable options, you'll not only have a more meaningful trip but also help ensure that this beautiful region remains a pristine haven for generations to come.

Chapter 21: Photography & Social Media Hotspots

Whether you're a seasoned photographer or just someone who loves to capture a moment for the 'gram, Zell am See offers some of the most picturesque settings in Europe. The landscapes here sprawling mountains, serene lakes, and quaint alpine villages seem to have been made for the perfect shot. And while the beauty of Zell am See is undeniably captivating, there are a few hidden gems and iconic spots that will make your camera or smartphone work overtime.

In this chapter, I'll share the must-visit locations for stunning photography, tips for capturing the essence of this beautiful town, and the best photography experiences you can enjoy during your visit.

21.1 Most Instagrammable Locations

Zell am See is a treasure trove of Instagrammable moments. The town, nestled between the shimmering Lake Zell and the majestic Hohe Tauern mountains, provides the perfect backdrop for both natural and urban photos. From the sparkling waters of the lake to the historic charm of the town, these spots will make your feed shine.

Lake Zell at Sunset

One of the most iconic shots you can get in Zell am See is at sunset. As the sun dips behind the mountains, the golden light casts a magical glow across the lake, creating a scene that is nothing short of mesmerizing. The reflections on the water are perfect for creating a mirror-like effect, and the surrounding snow-capped peaks add drama and majesty to your composition.

- **Where to Capture**: Head to Seepromenade for a lakeside stroll and find the perfect spot along the water's edge for that postcard-worthy photo.
- **Best Time**: Golden hour (about 30 minutes before sunset) will give you the soft, warm lighting that will transform your photo.

The View from Schmittenhöhe

For a bird's eye view of the entire region, the panoramic vistas from Schmittenhöhe, a mountain that towers over Zell am See, are unbeatable. The summit offers sweeping views of the town, the lake, and the surrounding mountain ranges. Whether you're taking in the landscape in the winter, when the peaks are blanketed in snow, or in summer, when the verdant meadows burst with color, the vista is always breathtaking.

- **Where to Capture**: The summit of Schmittenhöhe offers plenty of vantage points for capturing stunning landscape shots.

- **Best Time**: Early morning or late afternoon, when the lighting is softer and the crowds are thinner.

Zell am See's Old Town

The charm of Zell am See's historic center is a photographer's dream, filled with cobbled streets, quaint buildings, and colorful storefronts. The town is small, but its streets are lined with old-world architecture that contrasts beautifully against the natural backdrop of the mountains. The Church of St. Hippolytus, with its distinctive white facade, is a highlight and often appears in the foreground of many iconic photos of the town.

- **Where to Capture**: Wander around Bahnhofstrasse or the small alleys near the lakefront for charming, off-the-beaten-path shots.

- **Best Time**: Early morning, when the town is still quiet and the soft light illuminates the buildings.

Kaprun's Sigmund-Thun Klamm

Not far from Zell am See is Kaprun, home to the stunning Sigmund-Thun Gorge. The deep, dramatic gorge with its rushing waterfalls and the rugged rock formations make for a stunning photo op, especially with the vibrant green foliage during spring and summer. The pathways along the gorge lead you across wooden bridges and through tunnels, providing ample opportunities to snap dramatic, nature-focused shots.

- **Where to Capture**: Along the pathways and bridges in the gorge, capturing the water as it crashes over rocks, or framing the steep cliffs on either side.
- **Best Time**: Early afternoon when the sun casts the gorge in warm, dappled light.

21.2 Best Times & Angles for Capturing Stunning Photos

Timing is everything when it comes to photography, and in a place like Zell am See, understanding the best times of day and angles for shooting can make a world of difference.

Golden Hour: The Perfect Time for Magic

Golden hour the time just after sunrise and just before sunset, is arguably the best time to capture Zell am See's beauty in its most flattering light. The soft, warm glow of the sun enhances the colors of the town's architecture and the alpine landscape, giving everything a soft, ethereal quality. Early risers can also capture the serene, almost mystical light on the lake at sunrise, especially in winter when the town is dusted with snow.

- **Best Location for Golden Hour**: The shore of Lake Zell or the top of Schmittenhöhe.
- **Why It's Great**: The golden hues cast a dreamlike glow, making everything look magical, and the reflections on the water are absolutely stunning.

Blue Hour: After the Sun Sets

Blue hour, the period after sunset when the sky turns deep blue, is another incredible time to capture Zell am See's ambiance. The lights of the town begin to twinkle, and the cool tones of the sky contrast beautifully with the warm lights from the buildings. This is the perfect time for capturing the town's nightlife or the stillness of the lake after dark.

- **Best Location for Blue Hour**: From a vantage point above the town, such as Schmittenhöhe, or along Seepromenade.

- **Why It's Great**: The colors of the sky and the lights of the town create a mesmerizing contrast, offering a different perspective of Zell am See.

Framing the Landscape

One thing that makes Zell am See unique is how its landscape perfectly frames the town. Whether it's the towering peaks of the Hohe Tauern Mountains, the glassy surface of Lake Zell, or the quaint town center, there are endless opportunities for framing a perfect shot.

- **Best Location for Framing**: Find higher ground, such as Schmittenhöhe or the viewpoint near Kaprun, where the mountains and lake appear in the background of the town, giving your photos depth and scale.

- **Why It's Great**: These framed shots give a sense of place, emphasizing the connection between the town and its stunning natural surroundings.

21.3 Photography Tours & Workshops

For those who want to improve their photography skills or simply want a local's perspective on the best spots to capture, Zell am See offers a variety of photography tours and workshops.

These experiences allow you to learn from professionals, discover hidden gems, and return home with not only incredible photos but also valuable tips.

Guided Photography Tours

Several companies in Zell am See offer photography tours tailored to different skill levels. Whether you're a beginner looking for guidance on composition and lighting or a seasoned photographer seeking to perfect your technique, these tours are a great way to get a deeper understanding of the area while learning new skills.

- **What's Offered**: Tours typically include visits to the best photo spots in and around Zell am See, with a local guide helping you understand the nuances of capturing the landscape. Some tours even cater to specific types of photography, such as nature or architectural photography.

Photography Workshops

If you want a more immersive learning experience, consider taking a photography workshop during your stay. These workshops dive deep into techniques like landscape photography, long exposure shots, and editing your photos to enhance their impact.

- **Where to Book**: Look for workshops offered by local photographers or tourism offices.

They often provide small-group sessions where you can get personal feedback and assistance.

Zell am See is a photographer's paradise, offering everything from serene lake views to majestic mountains and charming alpine streets. Whether you're a seasoned photographer or someone who just loves capturing beautiful moments, the natural beauty of the region will leave you inspired. By knowing the best spots to visit, the optimal times for shooting, and the available workshops and tours, you can ensure that your photos reflect the essence of this breathtaking destination. So, pack your camera, head out with your eyes wide open, and capture the magic of Zell am See one frame at a time.

Chapter 22: What to Avoid & Common Travel Mistakes

Traveling is an exhilarating experience, one that opens you up to new sights, sounds, and cultures. But it's also easy to make mistakes, especially if you're in a foreign place for the first time. Zell am See, with its stunning landscapes and charming alpine town, is a true gem, but even the most seasoned travelers can fall into some common traps. From overpriced attractions to cultural faux pas, knowing what to avoid can help you get the most out of your trip without the stress or regret of unnecessary missteps.

In this chapter, I'll guide you through the things you should steer clear of in Zell am See, from tourist traps to cultural misunderstandings. I'll also share some practical advice on how to handle travel mishaps with grace, so your time here can remain as smooth and enjoyable as possible.

22.1 Overpriced Attractions & Tourist Traps

Zell am See is no stranger to its fair share of tourists, and while it's easy to get caught up in the excitement of seeing well-known sights, it's equally important to be aware of some common tourist traps.

The "Must-See" Yet Overpriced Ski Resorts

If you're visiting during the winter, Zell am See's ski resorts are one of the first things people rave about. And while the slopes are undoubtedly beautiful, the costs can add up quickly. Ski passes can be quite pricey, especially if you're only spending a day or two on the slopes, and some of the mountain restaurants charge sky-high prices for simple meals.

- **What to Avoid**: Don't fall for the "all-inclusive" ski packages unless you plan to be on the slopes for a full week or more. Instead, opt for a more flexible day pass or look into a combined pass that includes multiple resorts in the region for a better deal.

- **Travel Tip**: If you're not an avid skier, consider visiting during the off-season (spring or fall) when the prices drop significantly, and the town is less crowded, but still offers stunning views of the Alps.

Expensive Souvenir Shops

As with any popular tourist destination, Zell am See has a fair number of souvenir shops catering to travelers looking for a memento. While these shops can be fun to browse, the prices can often be inflated, particularly in the main square or near popular attractions like the lakefront.

You'll find many mass-produced items, from plush toys to postcards, but they often come with a hefty markup.

- **What to Avoid**: Don't spend too much in the tourist-heavy areas. Instead, explore the local markets or smaller, independent shops where you can find unique handmade goods at a better price. The local stores tucked away in Kaprun or the quieter corners of Zell am See offer authentic, locally crafted products.

22.2 Cultural Taboos & Mistakes to Avoid

Understanding the local culture and etiquette is crucial when visiting a foreign country, especially in places like Austria where traditions run deep. While Austrians are generally warm and welcoming to visitors, there are a few cultural nuances you should be aware of to avoid any unintentional offense.

Don't Underestimate the Importance of Punctuality

In Austria, punctuality is highly valued. Whether you're meeting friends for coffee or attending a guided tour, being on time is seen as a sign of respect. Showing up late, especially to a formal event or appointment, can be seen as inconsiderate or unprofessional.

- **What to Avoid**: Don't expect to "just show up" late to any event or appointment. Always plan to arrive at least 5–10 minutes early.

- **Travel Tip**: If you're taking a tour, make sure to be on time, as guides typically stick to a strict schedule. If you're late, you might find yourself missing out on part of the experience.

The Dress Code for Dining Out

While Zell am See is a laid-back town, it's still important to be mindful of dress codes when dining out, particularly at more upscale restaurants or in the evening. In general, Austrians tend to dress well when they go out, and overly casual attire may feel out of place in certain settings.

- **What to Avoid**: Avoid wearing flip-flops, tank tops, or overly casual clothing to fine dining establishments or in the evening.

- **Travel Tip**: When in doubt, go for smart-casual attire. A nice pair of trousers or a neat dress is perfect for dinner. In mountain resorts, the attire can be more relaxed, but you'll still want to dress appropriately when dining in more upscale spots.

Respecting Local Traditions and Customs

Zell am See and the surrounding regions have a deep connection to their traditions, including local festivals, food, and rituals. While most locals are understanding of tourists, it's still important to respect these cultural practices. For instance, Austrians are generally very respectful when it comes to personal space and may find overly familiar behavior from strangers a bit invasive.

- **What to Avoid**: Avoid touching personal belongings or acting too familiar with locals you don't know well. Also, be sure to respect any signs asking for silence or for guests to follow specific rules in cultural or religious settings.

- **Travel Tip**: If you attend a local event, take time to learn about the traditions or customs of the festival. It's a wonderful way to enrich your experience and show respect for the local culture.

22.3 Travel Mishaps & How to Prevent Them

Travel mishaps are inevitable, but they don't have to ruin your trip. Knowing how to handle some of the most common travel problems in Zell am See can help you stay calm and continue to enjoy your vacation.

Losing Your Way in the Mountains

The stunning mountain scenery can be disorienting, especially if you're hiking or exploring unfamiliar trails. Zell am See is surrounded by natural beauty, but navigating its hiking paths or even finding the right bus can be tricky for first-time visitors.

- **What to Avoid**: Don't wander off into the mountains without a map or without checking your route. Make sure you have a charged phone, and if you're planning to hike, always let someone know your route and estimated return time.

- **Travel Tip**: Always carry a map of the hiking trails or use a GPS app designed for hikers. There are plenty of easy-to-follow routes, and local guides are available to ensure you're safe.

Weather Surprises

Zell am See is known for its unpredictable mountain weather, with sudden rain showers or temperature drops, particularly in spring and fall. It's easy to be caught off guard if you're unprepared for the elements.

- **What to Avoid**: Don't assume the weather will stay sunny and warm all day. Always pack layers, and keep a rain jacket handy, just in case.

- **Travel Tip**: Check the weather forecast before you head out for the day. If you plan on skiing or hiking, ask your hotel or guide about the current conditions, especially if the weather seems unstable.

Dealing with Language Barriers

Though most people in Zell am See speak English, it's still a good idea to learn a few basic German phrases to help you get by. While Austrians are friendly and patient with tourists, speaking their language, even just a little, can go a long way in making you feel more comfortable.

- **What to Avoid**: Avoid assuming that everyone speaks English fluently, especially in rural areas. While most locals are accommodating, it's always best to make an effort with simple phrases like "Guten Morgen" (Good Morning) or "Wie geht's?" (How are you?).
- **Travel Tip**: If you're unsure of something, it's always polite to ask, "Sprechen Sie Englisch?" (Do you speak English?). Most people will appreciate the effort, and you'll likely get a much friendlier response.

Travel is about making memories, but avoiding common mistakes can ensure that those memories are positive ones.

Zell am See is a stunning destination, and with a little preparation, you'll not only avoid the tourist traps and cultural missteps but also experience the authentic heart of the town. Whether it's being punctual, respecting local customs, or preventing travel mishaps, a little awareness goes a long way. By following these tips, you'll be able to immerse yourself in the beauty of Zell am See without any of the stress, leaving you with nothing but fond memories.

Chapter 23: Departure & Final Travel Tips

As your time in Zell am See comes to an end, you may find yourself reluctant to say goodbye to the stunning mountain views, charming streets, and the warm hospitality of this picturesque town. However, even as your departure looms, there's still plenty to enjoy. Whether it's grabbing some last-minute souvenirs, ensuring you have everything packed, or making the most of your final moments in this alpine paradise, this chapter is your guide to wrapping up your Zell am See adventure with ease and grace.

I've crafted this section to help you navigate the final stages of your trip smoothly, offering practical tips for last-minute shopping, packing, and ensuring your departure goes off without a hitch. After all, your final day is just as important as the first and it should be just as enjoyable.

23.1 Last-Minute Shopping & Packing Checklist

Before you leave Zell am See, make sure you've picked up all the souvenirs, gifts, and items you'll cherish to remind you of your time here. The last day can often be a whirlwind of packing and last-minute purchases, but with a bit of planning, you can make it a relaxed and enjoyable experience.

Souvenirs to Remember Zell am See

Whether you're looking for a keepsake for yourself or a thoughtful gift for a loved one, Zell am See has a variety of charming shops offering unique items. Some of the best souvenirs are those that reflect the region's culture and natural beauty.

- **Handcrafted Items**: Zell am See is known for its local craftsmanship, from hand-carved wooden figurines to beautifully woven textiles. These pieces make perfect gifts or souvenirs that capture the essence of the town.

- **Alpine Apparel**: You'll find traditional Austrian alpine clothing such as dirndls and lederhosen, but also stylish winter wear perfect for colder climates. These high-quality garments are not only practical but are also a lovely reminder of your time in the Alps.

- **Local Products**: Take home some authentic Austrian treats like Mozartkugeln (Mozart balls), artisanal honey, or hand-pressed oils. You'll also find local wines and schnapps, which are a great way to bring a taste of Austria back with you.

Packing Checklist

As you pack for your return, it's important to ensure that you haven't left anything behind, and that your luggage is ready for the journey ahead. Use the following checklist to help you stay organized:

- **Documents & Essentials**: Double-check your passport, travel tickets, hotel reservations, and any other important documents. It's a good idea to keep these in a separate folder for easy access.

- **Electronics & Chargers**: Don't forget chargers for your phone, camera, or any other devices you used during your trip. It's also a smart move to back up photos and videos from your phone or camera to ensure you don't lose any precious memories.

- **Weather-Appropriate Clothing**: Zell am See's weather can change rapidly, so make sure you've packed for all conditions. If you're heading back to a warmer destination, remember to swap your ski gear for lighter clothing.

Travel Tip: As you're packing, be mindful of any travel regulations regarding liquids, especially if you bought any local alcohol or oils. Also, ensure you have adequate space for the souvenirs you've picked up!

23.2 Getting to the Airport or Train Station

By now, you're likely aware of the various transportation options that will take you to your departure point. Whether you're flying out of Salzburg or Innsbruck or catching a train from Zell am See, it's important to plan your journey to the airport or train station with enough time to spare.

By Train:

The Zell am See train station is well connected to major cities like Salzburg, Munich, and Vienna. Trains are comfortable, reliable, and offer a scenic route through the mountains making your journey feel like one last beautiful experience before you leave.

- **Train Tip**: Arrive at the train station at least 15–20 minutes before your train departs. This gives you time to find your platform and buy any last-minute snacks for the journey. The train station has several small shops where you can pick up local pastries or beverages to enjoy along the way.

By Bus or Car:

If you're catching a flight from Salzburg, Innsbruck, or even Vienna, you may want to take a bus or drive. For those who opt for the bus, the local bus station in Zell am See is well-connected to the larger cities.

- **Travel Tip**: Be sure to confirm your bus schedule in advance, as routes may change or have limited availability depending on the time of year. Always allow extra time for travel, particularly in winter months when snow and ice can cause delays.

Private Transfers:

If you're looking for a more luxurious and convenient way to leave Zell am See, consider booking a private transfer. These services can take you directly from your accommodation to the airport or train station, saving you time and hassle, especially if you have a lot of luggage or are traveling with family.

- **Travel Tip**: Book your transfer in advance, and make sure to reconfirm the details a day before your departure. Many services can be arranged through your hotel or through local transport companies.

23.3 Making the Most of Your Final Day

Your final day in Zell am See is the perfect opportunity to enjoy a few last moments in the town before you leave. Here are some suggestions to make the most of your final hours:

Take One Last Stroll Around the Lake

One of the best ways to end your trip is by taking a peaceful walk around Lake Zell. The crisp mountain air, the serene waters, and the breathtaking views of the surrounding Alps are sure to leave you with lasting memories of your time in this beautiful region.

- **Why It's Special**: The lake is especially beautiful in the early morning or late afternoon when the light is soft and the crowds are thinner. If you can, try to catch a glimpse of the lake at sunset it's truly magical.

Enjoy a Farewell Meal

Before you leave, indulge in one last Austrian meal. Zell am See has no shortage of cozy, welcoming restaurants where you can savor hearty alpine dishes. Whether you opt for a schnitzel, a warm bowl of Tiroler Gröstl (a traditional Austrian dish made with potatoes and meat), or fresh fish from the lake, take the time to enjoy your final meal as a reflection of your time in the region.

- **Recommendation**: Head to a traditional restaurant or tavern for a cozy, relaxed meal. The locals love their food, and it's a perfect way to say goodbye to the town with a satisfying taste of Austrian cuisine.

Capture Your Final Moments

Before heading out, don't forget to snap some final pictures. Whether it's a photo of you by the lake, a close-up of the mountains, or a final shot of the cobblestone streets in the town center, these photos will serve as lasting memories of your trip. Take a moment to reflect on everything you've experienced, from the outdoor adventures to the charming local experiences.

- **Photography Tip**: If you've taken a lot of photos throughout your trip, take a few moments to reflect and organize them on your phone or camera. That way, you'll have them neatly stored before you embark on your journey home.

Leaving Zell am See is never easy, but by following these final travel tips, you can ensure a smooth and memorable departure. Whether you're packing up your souvenirs, heading to the station, or savoring one last Austrian meal, your final moments in this alpine haven will leave you with a sense of fulfillment and peace. Every journey ends, but the memories you create along the way will stay with you forever.

Safe travels, and I hope your time in Zell am See has left you with stories to tell, photos to treasure, and a longing to return one day.

Chapter 24: Appendix & Additional Resources

As you prepare to explore Zell am See, having the right resources at your fingertips can make all the difference. Whether you need assistance with translation, are on the hunt for some hidden gems, or simply want to know the best times to visit, this chapter serves as your ultimate guide to navigating the practical side of your journey.

Think of it as the "toolkit" that complements the detailed travel narrative you've already enjoyed. In this section, I've gathered the most useful information to enhance your experience, ensuring that you feel well-equipped for any aspect of your trip.

24.1 Recommended Books, Websites & Travel Blogs

Before you pack your bags, consider diving into a few resources that can offer more depth to your trip. Whether it's about the region's history, local culture, or insider tips, the following books, websites, and travel blogs will help you go beyond the basics and immerse yourself fully in the destination.

Books

- The Alps: A Human History from Hannibal to the Present by Stephen O'Shea: This book delves deep into the historical and cultural significance of the Alps, perfect for understanding the landscape around Zell am See.

- Austrian Cuisine: A Culinary Journey by Rebekah Fox: Explore Austrian food through a culinary lens with this guide, which will give you new perspectives on the dishes you're likely to encounter during your visit.

Websites & Travel Blogs

- Zell am See-Kaprun Tourism: The official tourism website for Zell am See is a goldmine of information, offering up-to-date details on events, activities, and things to do.

- Austria.info: The official website of the Austrian National Tourist Office, packed with travel advice, destination highlights, and tips for navigating the country.

- The Alpine Explorer Blog: A travel blog that provides firsthand experiences, itineraries, and photography from the Austrian Alps, making it a fantastic resource for finding off-the-beaten-path gems in Zell am See.

These resources will not only provide additional insights into the places you'll visit but will also enhance your understanding of the region's rich heritage and vibrant present.

24.2 Essential Phrases in the Local Language

While many people in Zell am See speak English, it's always appreciated when visitors make an effort to speak the local language German. Here's a helpful list of essential phrases that can make your interactions more personal and immersive.

Basic Greetings & Phrases

- **Hello** – Hallo (informal), Guten Tag (formal)
- **Goodbye** – Auf Wiedersehen or Tschüss (informal)
- **Please** – Bitte
- **Thank you** – Danke
- **Excuse me** – Entschuldigung
- **How much is this?** – Wie viel kostet das?
- **Do you speak English?** – Sprechen Sie Englisch?
- **Where is the train station?** – Wo ist der Bahnhof?

These phrases will be particularly useful when navigating restaurants, shops, and asking for directions.

24.3 Emergency Contacts & Local Helplines

Emergencies can happen anywhere, and Zell am See is no exception. It's always best to be prepared with a list of local contacts in case something goes wrong during your travels. Here's a list of essential numbers and resources you may need while in Zell am See:

Emergency Numbers

- **General Emergency (Fire, Police, Ambulance)**: 112
- **Police Station Zell am See**: +43 6542 7000
- **Ambulance**: 144
- **Mountain Rescue (Alpine emergencies)**: 140

Medical Facilities

- **Zell am See Hospital (Krankenhaus Zell am See)**: +43 6542 7030
- **Pharmacy (Apotheke)**: Apotheke am Stadtplatz - +43 6542 7240

Having this information at your fingertips will help ensure you feel safe and prepared, no matter the situation.

24.4 Addresses of Major Landmarks, Attractions, and Important Locations

Knowing where key sites are located will help you make the most of your time in Zell am See. This section provides the addresses of essential places you won't want to miss.

Tourist Information Centers

- **Zell am See Tourist Information**: Brucker Bundesstraße 1, 5700 Zell am See

Museums, Parks, and Monuments

- **Zell am See Old Town**: Zentrum, 5700 Zell am See – A charming area full of medieval architecture.

- **Schmittenhöhe**: Schmittenhöhe 1, 5700 Zell am See – The main mountain offering stunning views and skiing in winter.

- **Kaprun Castle (Burg Kaprun)**: Kaprun 1, 5710 Kaprun – A historic landmark with breathtaking views of the surrounding Alps.

Recommended Restaurants & Cafes

- **Steinerwirt 1493**: Sigmund-Thun-Straße 27, 5700 Zell am See – A beloved restaurant offering hearty Austrian fare.

- **Zum Hirschen**: Kirchbichlstraße 26, 5700 Zell am See – A traditional Austrian spot known for its cozy atmosphere and delicious local dishes.

Hotels, Hostels, and Local Lodging Options

- **Schloss Prielau**: Prielau 6, 5700 Zell am See – A luxury hotel situated in a fairytale castle.

- **Hotel Tirolerhof**: Seespitzstraße 7, 5700 Zell am See – A charming lakeside hotel offering fantastic spa services.

- **Jugendherberge Zell am See**: Salzgasse 12, 5700 Zell am See – A budget-friendly option for young travelers.

Transportation Hubs

- **Zell am See Railway Station**: Bahnhofplatz 1, 5700 Zell am See

- **Zell am See Bus Station**: Bahnhofstraße 3, 5700 Zell am See

Shopping Districts, Souvenir Shops, and Markets

- **Zell am See Main Street**: The heart of Zell am See shopping, lined with boutiques and local shops offering handcrafted goods and regional treats.

- **Zell am See Farmers Market**: Tuesdays and Fridays at the town square, where you can pick up fresh local produce, cheeses, and other local products.

Medical Facilities & Pharmacies

- **Apotheke am Stadtplatz**: Stadtplatz 2, 5700 Zell am See – A pharmacy offering general healthcare supplies.

- **Zell am See Medical Center**: Brucker Bundesstraße 1, 5700 Zell am See – The main medical facility in town.

Emergency Services & Police Stations

- **Zell am See Police Station**: Brucker Bundesstraße 5, 5700 Zell am See

24.5 Local Holidays & Festivals Calendar

Austria, and Zell am See in particular, is full of lively festivals and holidays that celebrate everything from local culture to the changing seasons. Here's a brief overview of some of the key events to look out for during your visit:

- **New Year's Day (January 1)**: Celebrate the new year in style with local festivities and fireworks.

- **Ski Season Opening (December)**: Ski lovers gather in Zell am See for the grand opening of the ski season.

- **Zell am See Summer Festival (July–August)**: A vibrant celebration of music, dance, and local traditions.

- **Almabtrieb (Late September)**: A beautiful, traditional event where cows are brought down from the high pastures for the winter.

24.6 Helpful Travel Apps and Websites

To make your trip even easier, consider downloading a few travel apps that can help you navigate Zell am See, from transportation options to restaurant bookings and sightseeing tours.

- **Google Maps**: Essential for getting around and finding places to visit.

- **ÖBB Scotty**: The official app for Austrian public transportation, allowing you to check train and bus schedules.

- **TripAdvisor**: For recommendations on things to do, restaurants, and activities from fellow travelers.

- **WeatherPro**: A highly reliable weather app that will keep you updated on the forecast for outdoor adventures in the Alps.

This chapter has provided a wide range of resources to help you make the most of your time in Zell am See. From practical tips on what to do in an emergency to finding the best places to shop and dine, these tools will ensure that your journey is smooth and enjoyable. Now that you're equipped with these resources, you're ready to enjoy your adventure to its fullest, whether it's exploring the picturesque landscapes, delving into Austrian culture, or relaxing at a cozy café by the lake. Safe travels, and enjoy every moment of your time in Zell am See!

Printed in Dunstable, United Kingdom